15.25

3/96

WG

-2001

)01

01

)6

er cof fy mam

Age and Dignity:
Working with Older People

Neil Thompson

arena

Published by
Arena
Ashgate Publishing Limited
Gower House
Croft Road
Aldershot
Hants GU11 3HR
England

Ashgate Publishing Company
Old Post Road
Brookfield
Vermont 05036
USA

British Library Cataloguing in Publication Data

Thompson, Neil
  Age and Dignity: Working with
  Older People
  I. Title
  362.6

Library of Congress Catalog Card Number: 95–79849

ISBN 1 85742 251 1 (paperback)
ISBN 1 85742 250 3 (hardback)

Typeset in 10 on 12 pt Palatino by Photoprint, Torquay, Devon and printed in Great Britain by Hartnoll Ltd, Bodmin.

Contents

Foreword

In the 1990s, work with older people has taken on a new significance in terms of both social and health care. At least four reasons may be cited for the increasing concern being shown regarding the quality of activity in this area. First, demographic change has been one major element, with increased recognition of the central role played by older people in a range of social institutions. Second, services for older people are now the subject of wide debate, with critical issues arising from the implementation of the 1990 National Health Service and Community Care Act. Third, elderly people are themselves a more active group in society. They play a key role as carers for older and younger members of the community; they are active in a range of leisure and educational activities; and they are a key group in the redefinition of the life course, with the emerging distinction between the third and fourth age. Finally, the study of old age has itself been radically changed over the past ten years. A critical gerontology has been developed to highlight what its proponents see as the social construction of later life: that is, the influence of social institutions in defining dominant images and experiences of the ageing process.

Neil Thompson's important study builds on all the above themes, relating them to some of the crucial issues faced by professional carers in social and health services. In doing so, Thompson uses some of the key conceptual themes developed by critical perspectives in the study of the ageing. In particular, he makes extensive use of the critique of ageism, applying this to a range of contexts in which professionals are engaged. Thompson's study highlights the extent to which traditional work with older people has tended to neglect the impact of ageism on the lives of older people. Hence the importance of the model of anti-ageist practice which Thompson develops at the end of this study. This brings together a range of key issues for good practice and will be highly relevant to many professional groups involved in work with elderly people.

In conclusion, the lessons contained in this study have broad applicability; moreover, they are of added significance given the problems facing older people in the 1990s. Budgetary and related pressures may serve to reinforce stereotypes relating to old age. Texts such as *Age and Dignity* will play an important role in the struggle to develop a more liberated practice in work with older people. The issues it raises are central to the kind of health and social care we should be trying to build as we move into the next century.

Chris Phillipson
Professor of Applied Social Studies and Social Gerontology
University of Keele

Preface

Working with older people is an aspect of human service work that presents many demands but also offers considerable rewards. For those who see such work as routine and uninteresting, a world of challenges, commitment, mutual respect, responsiveness, job satisfaction and profound enjoyment remains a closed door. Ageism portrays older people as being of little social worth, of little value to anyone, and therefore unworthy of any investment of time, energy or commitment beyond what is strictly necessary. If people who work with the older age group cannot see through this myth, cannot recognize how destructive, demeaning and oppressive it is, then there is a very real danger that their practice will not do justice to the older people they aim to serve – in fact, I would argue that there is a very high chance that such an uninformed approach to practice will be very dangerous and have little regard for dignity, rights or empowerment. Indeed, a primary aim of this book is to challenge traditional practices that pay little or no heed to the dangers of ageism and therefore run the risk of condoning, reinforcing or exacerbating the destructive effects of ageist attitudes, practices and structures.

Older people are our 'future selves' and so we must recognize that allowing the perpetuation of ageism is not only an injustice for today's older people, it is also a sentence passed on future older generations, ourselves included. This book should therefore be seen as part of a broader movement to draw attention to discrimination and oppression, and identify strategies for providing more appropriate services and interventions when working with particular social groups. It is to be hoped, then, that a greater awareness of ageism and its insidiously harmful effects on older people will enable us to move forward towards a society less ready to dismiss groups of people that it sees as not being central to the very basis of society.

This book will not provide simple solutions, but should go some considerable way towards equipping staff who work with older people to recognize the significance of ageism and develop forms of practice that promote dignity through a process of challenging and countering ageism in all its forms and manifestations.

We live in a society that teaches each new generation that older people are of little value and have little to offer. It is not surprising, then, that we should start from a position in which such a perspective is reflected in our attitudes and actions. None the less, once we become aware of the damage that ageism does to older people, it should be quite clear that steps need to be taken to move beyond this starting point and make a positive contribution to developing experiences of old age characterized by dignity, equality and empowerment.

The book is written for the variety of people who work with older people, including health care and paramedical workers, social workers and social care staff. It is not directed at one specific group of staff, and should therefore offer something to all involved in working with older people.

Acknowledgements

I am very grateful to Professor Chris Phillipson of Keele University for kindly providing the foreword. Thanks are also due to Colin Richardson, Fellow of Keele University, John Bates and Alan Preston of North East Wales Institute of Higher Education (NEWI) and Susan Thompson for helpful comments on earlier drafts of the typescript. I am also pleased to acknowledge the help of Richard Pugh of NEWI with regard to Chapter 6 on dementia, as many of the ideas in that chapter derive from my experience of joint teaching with Richard on this subject. Once again, my thanks are due to Joyce Thompson for her efforts in typing the scripts.

Introduction

Working with older people has traditionally been seen as routine and relatively undemanding, requiring only basic training (Buckle, 1981; Barclay, 1982). A basic aim of this book is to challenge this notion by demonstrating the complexities, challenges and demands of working with older people – and by helping health and social welfare staff to respond positively and effectively to them.

I shall argue that the traditional approach is not simply a reflection of a lack of understanding of this type of work. It reflects a more deeply ingrained negative and dismissive view of older people. That is, it is an example of ageism. This is a central concept and one that is discussed in greater detail in Chapter 1. It helps us to recognize that, in working with older people, we are working with a group of people who experience disadvantage and discrimination.

In view of this, an important message of this book is that it is essential for staff to practise in a way which not only avoids reinforcing such discrimination and disadvantage, but also goes some way towards challenging and undermining them. Good practice must be anti-discriminatory practice (Thompson, 1993). This point will become a recurring theme throughout the book, and one which will be developed in more detail.

Another important theme to be developed is that working with older people is, after all, about working with people. This is a simple but none the less crucial point, and one often neglected. This is reflected in the language commonly used to refer to older people. Fennell *et al.* (1988) recognize the significant role of language and its potential for 'dehumanization', that is, treating people as things:

> One simple example is the stigmatizing use of adjectives as nouns. We try, wherever possible, not to talk of 'the elderly', 'geriatrics' (as applied to people),

1

'the confused'; but when we do have to generalize, we refer to 'elderly people', 'older people', 'ill people', 'people in old age' or 'confused elderly people'. This is not to deny the physical realities of ageing, disability or dementia, but to try, linguistically, to remind ourselves constantly of human variety in the groups we are categorizing and to underline the 'people-status' (people like us, in other words) of elderly people as opposed to the 'thing-status' (objects inferior to us) of 'the elderly'. (pp. 7–8)

Similarly, Hughes and Mtezuka (1992), in their discussion of social work with older women, comment on the way demeaning words or phrases are commonly used by staff in addressing their clients:

at the level of communication with older women, the way in which the practitioner approaches and talks to the older woman will reflect a belief in her right to respect and autonomy. There can be no place, then, for addressing old women by their first names without permission; for using infantilizing or stereotypical labels such as 'granny' or 'old dear'; for treating or speaking to the person in any way which symbolically reflects an abuse of power or an invasion of their privacy or rights. (p. 236)

We therefore have to be careful about the language we use in order to ensure that we do not contribute to the tendency to dehumanize older people. Or, to put it another way, the dignity of older people is something to be preserved and promoted rather than undermined.

Another aspect of recognizing the humanity of older people is the need to acknowledge the artificial barriers we impose. For example, the notion of 'crisis' plays an important role in understanding social work and health care, and yet it is one which is often neglected in working with older people:

Ratna (1990) bemoans the tendency to exclude elderly people from the purview of crisis intervention. Old age is often (wrongly) seen as a 'contra-indication' for crisis work and yet, he argues, some form of crisis is the main reason for admission to care. (Thompson, 1991, p. 120)

This is characteristic of a broader tendency to assume that theories and methods of intervention used with other age groups are not applicable to older people. It is as if older people are not considered to be worth the investment of time, effort and energy. Indeed, this can be seen to represent a further aspect of ageism, that of 'marginalization', the process by which older people are pushed to the margins of society and their interests are disregarded. Working with older people in a routine and unimaginative way both reflects this marginalization and reinforces it. This is a key point which underpins the arguments put forward in Chapter 5.

The need to treat older people as people seems so obvious and yet it is so often forgotten in the day-to-day demands of practice. In its mildest form, this amounts to a routine, mechanistic and impersonal treatment of the older people we work with. At its most severe, it amounts to 'elder abuse', a serious form of ill-treatment in which vulnerable older people are exploited or harmed. The tendency to dehumanize elderly people is therefore one that will be strongly challenged in this book.

Older people form a social group in their own right and therefore have their own specific needs. For our work to be effective and appropriate, it is essential that we are sensitive to these needs and the particular contexts in which they arise. An important message which emerges is the need to locate work with older people within the context of a broad range of factors – biological, psychological, social, political and philosophical. An important feature of this book, therefore, is the exploration of these various factors and a consideration of their significance.

One important further aspect of this context is that of demography – the study of population trends. The distribution of age groups within British society is in the course of a major process of change. In particular, what is occurring is a growth in what Marshall (1990) refers to as 'old old' people (those over the age of 75), combined with a relative decline in 'young old' people (see Tinker, 1992, for more detailed information). This 'Rising Tide', as it is sometimes called, has significant implications for the provision of health and social welfare services. Specifically, we need to recognize the development of a 'care gap':

> We are witnessing a rapid increase in the higher age groups combined with a relative decline in the 'young elderly' group. This suggests a significant increase in the number of elderly people requiring care and attention but a decrease in the younger generation who would normally be expected to care for them. There will be a considerably elevated level of demand for services and a great deal of extra pressure on staff, so the way we manage services for elderly people is becoming increasingly important. (Thompson, 1989, p. ii)

What this means, in effect, is that the challenge of working with older people is a steadily increasing one. This is perhaps a mixed blessing. On the one hand, the extra pressure on staff and resources which are already over-burdened will not be a welcome addition. However, as the pressures grow, it will become increasingly difficult for work with older people to be dismissed as routine and undemanding, especially as the significance of, and need for, anti-ageist practice becomes more established.

The challenge of ageing is a significant one, as is the challenge of helping people combine old age with dignity. It is therefore important that staff and other carers are equipped for this challenge with an understanding of the key issues that arise. There are many such issues, and this book cannot hope to cover them all. However, it can at least begin the process of developing the knowledge and skills we need to ensure that old age and dignity go hand in hand.

The book is divided into eight chapters. The first sets the scene by exploring the significance of ageism and establishing the need to develop anti-ageist practice. Chapter 2 examines the ageing process, but goes far beyond the traditional approach with its narrow focus on biological processes and physical decline. It presents ageing as a much more complex phenomenon with many facets – psychological, social, political and philosophical.

Chapter 3 presents an overview of the main aspects of social policy relating to older people and highlights some of the implications of this policy context for practitioners. Chapter 4 is entitled 'Dealing with difficulties' and covers a range of common problems encountered in working with older people. Although no solutions to these problems can be guaranteed, potentially useful strategies for tackling them can be explored. Chapter 5 also has a practical focus, and has as its subject matter the actual tasks and duties staff face. In effect, the chapter poses two basic questions: What needs to be done? and What are the best ways of doing it?

Chapter 6 concentrates on issues relating to dementia. It seeks to clear up some common misunderstandings and encourages a positive approach to this demanding and distressing condition. This paves the way for Chapter 7 which examines the demands on carers, both in relation specifically to dementia and more generally to other care demands. This chapter suggests a number of ways in which carers can be supported.

Chapter 8 is the concluding chapter and it is here the key issues addressed in the book are summarized and knitted together into an overall perspective. From this a number of conclusions can be drawn and a 'charter' for anti-ageist practice sketched out.

1 Understanding ageism

Introduction

Ageism is an issue which is increasingly receiving attention and its full significance is gradually being appreciated. Whilst other forms of oppression such as racism and sexism are relatively well-established as significant issues for health and social welfare, ageism has yet to be recognized to the same extent. For example, the term is often used in inverted commas, as if it is not yet an official part of the English language.

This reflects the progress that has yet to be made in bringing to people's attention the negative effects of ageism and its destructive potential. Until there is a much higher level of awareness of ageism, older people will continue to be disadvantaged and discriminated against, very often by the very people who are caring for them. It is therefore important that we understand what ageism is, how it operates and how it can be challenged or undermined.

What is ageism?

For Fennell *et al.* (1988): 'Ageism means unwarranted application of negative stereotypes to older people. For example, it is common to assume that old age inevitably brings ill-health' (p. 97). Hughes and Mtezuka (1992) describe ageism in similar terms: 'Ageism is the social process through which negative images of and attitudes towards older people, based solely on the characteristics of old age itself, result in discrimination' (p. 220).

However, we can in fact go a step further than this by recognizing that older people constitute an oppressed group. The stereotypes and negative images can be seen to oppress older people in terms of:

5

- 'marginalization' – exclusion from mainstream society;
- the use of dismissive and demeaning language;
- humour and mockery;
- physical, sexual, emotional and financial abuse (see Chapter 4);
- economic disadvantage;
- restricted opportunities or 'life-chances'.

Regarding ageism as a form of oppression has two major implications:

1 Ageism is not simply a matter of personal prejudice – it has its roots in the way society is organized. This is a point I shall address in more detail below.
2 In working with older people, we must recognize that the starting point is one of disadvantage and discrimination, rather than equality. It is therefore necessary to develop anti-ageist practice. It is not enough to avoid ageism – we must also challenge it.

There is a strong parallel here with the social model of disability which presents disablement not simply as a physical impairment, but also as a form of social oppression. For example, the Union of the Physically Impaired Against Segregation (UPIAS) comment that:

> In our view, it is society which disables physically impaired people. Disability is something imposed on top of our impairments by the way we are unnecessarily isolated and excluded from full participation in society. To understand this it is necessary to grasp the distinction between the physical impairment and the social situation, called 'disability', of people with such impairment. Thus we define . . . disability as the disadvantage or restriction of activity caused by a contemporary social organisation which takes no or little account of people who have physical impairments and thus excludes them in the mainstream of social activities. Physical disability is therefore a particular form of social oppression. (1976, pp. 3–4)

A similar argument can be applied to older people. Old age is not, in itself, a major problem, but the way in which older people are portrayed and treated certainly is. It is therefore important to see old age in its broader social context. This point will be an important issue in Chapter 2 where the ageing process is discussed.

If, then, older people constitute an oppressed group, what implications does this have for practice? Perhaps the most significant implication is the need to recognize the danger of condoning, reinforcing or exacerbating that oppression. There is a danger that, if we are not aware of, and sensitive to, the workings of ageist oppression, our attitudes and actions can make the situation worse. That is, we can be part of the problem, rather than part of the solution (Thompson, 1992a).

Practice focus 1.1

Joan had worked with older people for a number of years in a variety of residential settings. She had always prided herself on how well she treated the people she cared for. However, after attending a workshop on anti-ageist practice, she became conscious that, in many ways, she had been contributing to ageism without realizing that she was doing so. In particular, she acknowledged that she had tended to concentrate on the basic physical needs of residents and had not considered issues of rights or choice.

A helpful way of understanding ageism is in terms of its three dimensions or levels – personal, cultural and structural. This forms the basis of 'PCS analysis' (Thompson, 1993). The three dimensions of ageism – personal (**P**), cultural (**C**) and structural (**S**) – are each important in their own right.

Personal (**P**)   Personal prejudice against older people is not uncommon. This can perhaps be linked to our own fear of ageing, our own reluctance to accept that we are finite beings – each day growing older. Indeed, the report of the Board for Social Responsibility (1990) presents fear of death as an important reason for ageism (see the discussion of 'ontology' in Chapter 2).

Cultural (**C**)   Although many people may be prejudiced, this is not enough to explain the prevalence of ageism in society. Personal prejudice is often a manifestation of a broader cultural level of ageism. That is, dominant cultural values and beliefs can be seen to reflect ageism. As Picton (1991) comments:

> Attitudes and values provide foundations for the beliefs that shape and guide our perceptions of, and responses to, social groups like the aged, the disabled and delinquents. If our responses are based on negative, stereotyped attitudes, the result is likely to be rejection and stigmatisation. (p. 10)

Stereotypes are a key feature of the cultural level as they play a central part in propagating and maintaining negative images. A basic aspect of culture and stereotypes is that they both operate 'beneath the surface'. They work in such a way as to become invisible and taken for granted – we do not notice they are there unless and until they are pointed out to us. For example, it is commonly assumed that old age and sexuality are not compatible, and yet this can be clearly shown not to be the case (Gibson, 1992).

The cultural level also manifests itself in two other significant ways:

1 *Language*: As noted earlier, the language used to describe or address older people is often demeaning, depersonalizing or patronizing. A particular example of this is infantilization. This refers to the tendency to treat older people as if they were children – in the same way that sexist language refers to adult women as 'girls'. I shall return to this point below.

2 *Humour*: Although humour can be used positively to challenge stereotypes, older people are often the subject of mockery or destructive humour (Victor, 1994). For example, in 'sitcoms' older people are frequently portrayed in stereotypical terms as 'doddering old fools'. Whilst many people are now sensitive to racist and sexist humour, a much smaller proportion of people are attuned to the ageist nature of many jokes and forms of humour.

Structural (**S**)   The predominance of ageist attitudes and values at a cultural level is, of course, no coincidence – it is a reflection of the broader context of the structure of society. Ageist values both support and derive from power structures in society.

As a result of their departure from the labour market, older people tend to experience a loss of economic power. Because the production of material wealth is so highly valued in industrial societies, older people who are no longer active in the labour market are seen as a drain on resources and a burden for the wealth-producing majority:

> One of the groups to suffer is the elderly population, who are left: 'weak, crushed and powerless' (de Beauvoir, 1977, p. 310). Older people have their place in society defined for them by capitalist need, and become the victims of it. Phillipson (1989) suggests that radical social reform is needed so that capitalism is prevented from producing casualties, such as those it rejects on the grounds of age. (Thompson and Thompson, 1993, p. 17)

In a society motivated primarily by the production of wealth, older people as a group will be devalued and disempowered. Again there is a parallel here with disability, with disabled people who are outside of the labour market also being devalued and marginalized (Oliver, 1990). Simone de Beauvoir, in her detailed study of old age, neatly captures the central issue when she comments that:

> By the fate it allots to its members who can no longer work, society gives itself away – it has always looked upon them as so much material. Society confesses

that as far as it is concerned, profit is the only thing that counts, and that its 'humanism' is mere window-dressing. (1977, p. 603)

In order to understand ageism, then, it is necessary to appreciate the importance of each of these levels and the interrelationships between them. At one extreme, an over-exclusive focus on the personal dimension fails to take account of powerful cultural and social forces and therefore presents too confined and simplistic a picture. At the other extreme, a focus purely on the broader aspects of ageism loses sight of personal ownership, the part each of us plays in either reinforcing or challenging existing ageist structures and practices – it allows us to locate the problem outside our control. In short, it gives us an excuse not to address our own tendencies towards ageism.

Ageism and oppression

As a result of ageism, older people experience oppression in a number of ways. These include direct forms of oppression (for example, elder abuse) and more subtle and indirect forms (for example, the use of patronizing language). Awareness of such oppression is often very limited and reflects the tendency to marginalize matters of concern in relation to older people – itself an example of ageist ideology. Whilst public consciousness of oppressions such as racism and sexism can be seen to have grown over the years, ageism has not received anywhere near the same amount of attention.

Ageism is also more readily tolerated and accepted in society. For example, derogatory comments about age (old codger, daft old fool) are commonplace and tend to go unchallenged, whereas racist equivalents would be much more likely to provoke objections or disapproval – and, indeed, are much less likely to be uttered in the first place. This is a very significant issue as it means that there is a danger that a lack of awareness of ageism can lead to oppression being condoned, reinforced or exacerbated. If we are not sensitive to the ways in which ageism operates in oppressing older people, we run the risk, as mentioned earlier, of being part of the problem, rather than part of the solution. That is, staff working with older people can, through their attitudes and actions, either challenge and undermine oppression, or contribute to such oppression:

There is no middle ground; intervention either adds to oppression (or at least condones it) or goes some small way towards easing or breaking such oppression. In this respect, the political slogan, 'If you're not part of the solution, you must be part of the problem' is particularly accurate. (Thompson, 1992a, p. 169)

This is a significant point and one that is not always appreciated. A common response is to turn one's back on the issues and to dismiss them with a comment such as, 'It doesn't apply to me, I'm not prejudiced'. However, as we noted earlier, discrimination and oppression are not simply matters of personal prejudice (the **P** level), they also apply at the broader levels of culture and social structure. One very important implication of this is that ageism can result even when there is no intention to discriminate. Policies, structures and institutional practices can be experienced as oppressive even when the staff carrying them out are acting entirely in good faith.

A very significant distinction here is that between intentions and outcomes. Unless we are aware of the broader context of ageism, positive intentions can, none the less, produce negative outcomes. For example, the good intentions of staff in trying to 'look after' older people may produce dependency and feelings of resentment and low self-esteem.

Practice focus 1.2

When Joan became aware of ageism and how it had influenced her practice, she at first felt very guilty, as she realized she had contributed to reinforcing ageist stereotypes. Fortunately, a colleague was able to reassure her that she had acted in good faith and had not intended any harm. After further discussion, they were both able to recognize that good intentions can lead to negative outcomes. From this they were able to deduce that they would have to be very sensitive to the dangers of ageism in future, as good intentions are clearly not enough on their own.

In such cases, the ageism arises from the organizational context which fails to ensure the creation of an ethos of empowerment in which workers fully recognize the dangers of dependency and the need to help older people gain as much control over their lives as possible. This is a point to which I shall return below.

PCS analysis takes us some way towards a theory of ageism as a form of oppression. However, we also need to consider a number of other aspects, in particular, the ways in which such oppression manifests itself. Some of these have already been mentioned, for example, dehumanization and demeaning language. However, these are worthy of revisiting, alongside other examples of oppression not yet discussed.

Dehumanization

The tendency to dehumanize older people has been recognized as a significant feature of ageism. As de Beauvoir (1977) comments: 'Old age is particularly difficult to assume because we have always regarded it as something alien, a foreign species' (p. 315). A combination of a reluctance to face up to the finite nature of life and negative images of old age produces a tendency to shun old age and disregard its significance – we pretend it is not there and thereby fail to see it as part of 'normal' existence.

Dehumanization also manifests itself in terms of our expectations of older people. One characteristic of human existence is the need to find meaning and create meaningful plans and activities or, to use the technical term, existential projects. However, as far as older people are concerned, this characteristic is often assumed not to exist. For example, Biggs (1993) argues that the projects and endeavours of younger people are more highly valued in society than those of their older counterparts. This can be reflected in service provision where practical caring tasks can be emphasized at the expense of creating opportunities for meaningful action and interaction.

Dehumanization is also significant in terms of the use of demeaning language and the incidence of elder abuse, two examples of oppression worthy of attention in their own right.

Ageist language

I have argued previously (Thompson, 1994a) that language can be problematic in a number of ways:

> The subject of discriminatory language is a complex one but, as a general rule, you should avoid terms that:
>
> - exclude – 'every man for himself';
> - depersonalise – 'the elderly';
> - stigmatise – 'blackleg'. (p. 78)

Specifically in relation to older people, language can be overtly offensive – the list of derogatory terms referring to older people is a very long one indeed – and therefore quite stigmatizing. Terms such as 'the elderly', 'the old', 'EMI' are commonly used but are, none the less, very dehumanizing – they 'depersonalize' the people to whom they refer; language can also patronize older people through the use of terms such as 'old dear', or by using first names without checking that this is acceptable.

Language is an important 'social signifier', in the sense that the type and form of language we use is socially significant – it indicates power relationships, the presence or absence of respect, and our expectations of one another (Pugh, 1996). Language therefore plays a pivotal role with regard to dignity – it can either enhance it or act as a barrier to its realization.

The subject of sensitivity to language is one that is often trivialized and dismissed as 'political correctness'. However, this is a dangerous tendency and one that should be avoided. Language is a very powerful vehicle for transmitting dominant ideas and values and has the capacity to endorse, reinforce and exacerbate social inequalities, and so we have to be careful not to allow inappropriate language use to undermine our progress towards anti-ageist practice. Language that reflects and reinforces ageism can be a serious obstacle to ageism being recognized as a form of oppression to be avoided and challenged.

Elder abuse

Whilst child abuse has been a major issue for health and social welfare practice for some considerable time, the abuse of older people has received relatively little attention until recently, especially in Britain (Bennett and Kingston, 1993). The topic of elder abuse is considered in more detail in Chapter 4 and so I will not pursue the matter fully here.

It is worth noting, however, that the abuse of older people is a significant aspect of ageist oppression insofar as it involves an abuse of power against a relatively powerless group of people. It can be argued that a significant feature of abuse is that the marginalized and devalued position of older people in society 'sets the scene' for abuse by placing elders in a disadvantaged and disempowered position. That is, abuse can be seen not simply as an isolated matter unconnected with broader social forces. It is surely no coincidence that a relatively powerless group is subject to such abuses. It clearly has much to do with social structures and attitudes towards older people. As de Beauvoir (1977) comments:

> It is common knowledge that the condition of old people today is scandalous. Before examining it in detail, we must try to understand how it comes about that society puts up with it so easily. As a general rule society shuts its eyes to all abuses, scandals and tragedies, so long as these do not upset its balance; and it worries no more about the fate of the children in state orphanages, or of juvenile delinquents, or of the handicapped, than it does about that of the aged. (p. 243)

Infantilization

A further significant aspect of ageism is the treating of older people as if they were children, thereby placing them in a subordinate role. As Leonard (1984) comments:

> Perhaps because dependency is only fully legitimated in the parent–child hierarchy of the nuclear family, dependency in old age . . . is almost invariably associated with treating the elderly as if they were children. This infantilising process, where the elderly person's rights as an adult are stripped away and he or she is simply subjected to the will of others, appears to be widespread, not only among old people's own children, where familial role-reversal takes place, but also in the health and welfare interventions of the state. (p. 191)

This is often reflected in the way in which services are organized. For example, it is not uncommon for Social Services Departments to be subdivided into services for children; services for adults; and services for 'the elderly'. This is a reflection of what Midwinter (1990) calls 'postadulthood', a conception of old age as a stage beyond adulthood, a return to a position of childlike subordination – older people are not included in the category of 'adults'.

Infantilization is also reflected in some forms of language used (Hockey and James, 1993). For example, terms like 'the old boy' or 'the old girl' have distinctly childlike connotations. This illustrates the broader linguistic process in which oppressed groups are referred to as if they were children as, for example, in the use of 'girls' to refer to adult women, or 'boy' to refer to a black man.

Denial of citizenship

Taylor (1989) argues that: 'Citizenship has not been realised for excluded groups either through the false collectivism of social democratic welfare, or through the consumerist "democracy" of the market' (p. 19). Older people can be seen to be one such 'excluded group':

> Citizenship can be seen as the relationship between the individual and the state and so hinges on a set of rights and duties. The negative and derogatory images of older people implicit in ageism have the effect of lowering expectations in respect of both rights and duties. For example, in terms of rights, it is often assumed by carers of elderly people that social services departments have the right to remove elderly people to residential care on a compulsory basis because they are 'at risk'. Contrary to the dominance of such a belief elderly people do have the right to remain in their own homes regardless of the degree of risk to which they are exposed (except where the Mental Health Act 1983 or section 47 of the National Assistance Act 1948 apply). However, a right which is widely assumed not to exist is a severely weakened right. (Thompson, 1992b, p. 35)

This relates to the key issue of protection from risk. A paternalistic approach to older people places the emphasis on protecting them from risk of harm, without recognizing the costs involved in this in terms of the loss of rights, independence and dignity. Of course, older people have as much right to take risks as any other group of people.

Welfarism

Health and social welfare staff working with older people have a biased experience of old age insofar as we tend to focus on problems, difficulties and weaknesses as a result of working with the most vulnerable members of the older age group. We can easily lose track of the fact that this represents a relatively small proportion of the overall elderly population (Windmill, 1992). A propensity to see only the problems of old age is reinforced by negative ageist stereotypes:

> Of course, stereotypes are grounded in reality. No one can deny that some old people are sick, dependent, poor and lonely. Careful study of the facts, however, puts these people into a total context. But too often we tend to ignore the facts in favour of a distorted view presented by media, advertisers, governments, or even our own prejudices. (Picton, 1991, p. 11)

This biased, unduly negative, view of old age can lead to 'welfarism', a view of older people as being necessarily in need of welfare services, as if old age were itself a problem in its own right. Fennell *et al.* (1988) point out the danger of 'welfarizing' older people:

> There may be nothing wrong with welfare, as such, but there is a danger that the people we welfarize, we do not allow fully human stature. They are not quite whole people, not people like us . . . [T]o approach the study of old age in terms only of problems and needs involves what Johnson (1976) has rightly termed a pathology model. We are prevented from seeing the whole picture and focusing it correctly, we see elderly people only in terms of their diseases, disabilities and deprivations. We focus unerringly on poverty, bereavement, social isolation, loneliness, role loss, illness, handicap, apathy and abuse. (pp. 6–7)

It is therefore important to ensure that a combination of stereotypes and occupational bias do not lead to an overly negative conception of old age and older people.

Medicalization

Old age is often viewed in predominantly medical terms. Indeed, Bytheway and Johnson (1990) see biology as the basis of attempts to justify ageism:

> It is on the basis of biological differences, and in particular their visible manifestations, that people can be perceived to be of 'different kinds'. Just as it is biological variation which is employed to 'legitimate' distinctions on grounds of gender, disability and race, so it is the biology of the ageing process which is popularly perceived to justify beliefs about age. (p. 30)

This emphasis on the biological dimension of ageing is an important issue which will be addressed in Chapter 2. It is also used as a justification for equating old age with a period of illness and infirmity. Once again, this is an ageist distortion of the situation that actually applies:

> As a general rule it is true that the greater one's age, the higher the incidence of illness will be. However, this is a long way from the commonly held assumption that all or even most older people are ill. But, in reality, the extent of illness and infirmity in old age is grossly exaggerated. (Thompson, 1993, pp. 84–5)

It is important that this point is fully recognized. To treat older people as if they are in need of care and attention, simply because they are old, can be a considerable source of oppression and distress. Furthermore, the fact that an older person may need care and attention should not be equated with illness – and thereby bring all the 'trappings' that the 'sick role' can attract. This can be problematic in one of two ways. On the one hand, this approach may be resented and cause ill-feeling, openly or otherwise. On the other hand, the sick role may appeal to the person concerned and may be taken on board, thereby creating dependency and acting as a barrier to empowerment.

Practice focus 1.3

Mrs Fenwick was 86 when her grandson returned to live near her after having lived abroad for a number of years. At first, she was very pleased that he visited her regularly and took an interest in her welfare. However, after a little while his attitude began to wear her down. His anxiety about her health manifested itself as constant questions about how she was feeling. She experienced this as an unwelcome pressure and felt undermined by his perception of her as unwell. The matter came to a head one day when he telephoned her doctor, without first consulting his grandmother, to request a home visit. Mrs Fenwick's anger at this gave her the opportunity to talk to her grandson about his unhelpful attitude towards her.

Multiple oppressions

Whilst recognizing the significance of ageism as a form of oppression, we also need to understand how ageism relates to other oppressive forces such as sexism, racism and disablism. As we have seen, ageism has its roots in the way society is organized. It can therefore be seen to intersect with other aspects of social structure, other social divisions such as class and gender.

One clearly established linkage is that between age and socioeconomic class or, more specifically, poverty (Phillipson, 1982, 1989). These links have been intensified and highlighted by the growing dominance of New Right ideology with its emphasis on personal responsibility, particularly in relation to preparing for one's retirement – the growth of personal pension plans, combined with a reduction in state provision, for example (Thompson and Thompson, 1993).

One of the consequences of this emphasis on individualism is the amplification of class differences. Those people whose socioeconomic position allows them to invest heavily in their old age will have a distinct advantage in later life over those who are less well-equipped to do so. This class distinction is further reflected in the relationship between class, age and power. As noted above, old age is characterized, in general terms at least, by powerlessness and marginalization. However, balanced against this is the existence of a small but significant minority of older people who are in very powerful positions – councillors, MPs, the judiciary and so on. The distinguishing factor between the powerless majority and the powerful minority is, of course, that of class. The class background of the holders of power is a major factor as there are clearly established links between class membership and political and judicial power.

Norman (1985) also looks at issues of class and age but adds the further dimensions of race and ethnicity. She describes the interaction of the three aspects as a form of 'triple jeopardy'. Phillipson (1989) comments that this refers to the fact that ethnic minority elders:

> not only face discrimination because they are old; in addition, many of them live in disadvantaged physical and economic circumstances; finally they are likely to face discrimination because of their culture, language, skin colour or religious affiliation. (p. 203)

The marginalization resulting from low income is reinforced by the additional discriminatory impact of both racism and ageism.

The situation also needs to be considered from a demographic point of view. Chakrabarti (1990) points out the lack of attention paid to demography as it affects social policy and black people. He comments:

> Another factor the providers of social work service very seldom take into account is the demography of the black population in this country. As with all other public service provision, a lack of understanding of the nature and distribution of black people will inevitably lead to wrong or inappropriate policy formulation, which in turn will produce more dissatisfaction and injustice. (p. 29)

He goes on to relate this weakness more specifically to the more rapid growth in the older population and the services they are likely to need:

> only a small proportion of black people – about 6 per cent – are over retirement age (the overall national figure is about 18 per cent). However, this situation will start changing dramatically towards the end of the century, and it appears that very few public institutions are anywhere near taking this demographic factor into serious consideration with the context of relevant policy formulation. (p. 30)

The number of people affected by triple jeopardy will continue to rise, and so a failure on the part of policy makers and service providers to take this into account and plan appropriately can be seen as a discriminatory action – one of omission, rather than commission.

Ahmad-Aziz *et al.* (1992) also draw attention to the significance of racism for black elders, in conjunction with ageism:

> Ageism can occur at a personal, attitudinal and institutional level. It is the assumption that, because people are old, they are inevitably inferior, inadequate, or of low status. These attitudes may be expressed in behaviour, as ageism is pervasive in western industrial society. Elders are often accorded a status of little value, rendering their condition, need and wants either invisible or subject to ridicule . . . Many studies and reports provide evidence that racism is pervasive in the institutions with which elders may come into contact, in health, social services and local authority settings, in an organizational and personal framework (Rooney 1987, CRE/ADSS 1978). (p. 14)

Work with older people therefore needs to be sensitive to not only ageism but also racism, in order to ensure that services are ethnically sensitive (attuned to people's cultural needs) and anti-racist (geared towards challenging racial discrimination).

Discrimination on the grounds of gender can also combine with ageism to produce what Sontag (1978) terms the 'double standard of aging'. Ford and Sinclair (1989) comment:

> Women's experience of old age is both qualitatively and quantitatively different from that of men. While all older people are subject to the discriminatory and demeaning process of ageism, women suffer additional disadvantages because of their low status, their traditional role(s), their lack of economic power and because the majority of them live alone. (p. 74)

Once again there is a demographic dimension to this combination of oppressive forces. Peace (1986) points out that the vast majority of older people are women (over two-thirds of those over 75 years) and so the impact of sexism applies to a much wider proportion of this age group than the general population. The double disadvantage of ageism and sexism is well captured in the opening sentence of Peace's paper: 'It would appear that in our society old women are all around us and yet invisible – in that their existence is seldom acknowledged; their needs are seldom recognized and their voices seldom heard' (p. 61).

The situation of older women has even been neglected within the women's movement. Hughes and Mtezuka (1992) refer to the 'failure of feminism' and comment that:

> Feminism may be fairly accused not only of neglecting older women, but of reinforcing both the ageism and the sexism which affect their lives . . . one of the central features of the women's movement has been its campaign to construct images of womanhood which emphasize the strength and power of women. Women have been encouraged to shed the victim role in domestic, economic, social, and political life, to be assertive and to reject the images of weakness and dependency. But what meaning do these images offer to older women? By failing to embrace a multiplicity of images of womanhood, which would include and validate the frailty and dependency of some older women, feminists have cut themselves off from their own futures. (p. 221)

They also go on to argue that the women's movement assumes that the issues for younger women, and the advances made in relation to those issues, will be the same for older women. In short, the specific needs and circumstances of older women have not been taken into account.

We can take this a step further by considering, in addition, the race dimension. Ahmad-Aziz *et al.* (1992) capture this complex interplay of factors in the following passage:

> For Black elders who are women the situation may be even worse, as they are subject to the sexism experienced by many elderly women in a male-dominated society. Such a woman might experience a triple standard of discrimination, of sexism all her life, compounded by racism and ageism in her last years. Women who become frail may be seen as of little use, either sexually, or in terms of their assumed caring functions. Those Black women who are formal carers employed in institutions experience racism from clients and patients, sometimes in a most painful way. (p. 14)

A further combination of oppressions is that of ageism and disablism (Oliver, 1983, 1990) but here we must tread carefully. One common ageist assumption is that old age is characterized by frailty and disability. However, as Qureshi and Walker (1986) remind us, the vast majority of elderly people are able to cope unsupported and so we need to be wary of equating old age with disability.

None the less, for many older people some degree of physical impairment does lead to disability and so the discrimination and negative stereotyping of the able-bodied majority are experienced in addition to the oppressive effects of ageism. Indeed, ageism and disablism have much in common:

- a patronizing attitude;
- a tendency towards exclusion and marginalization;
- negative images and stereotyping;
- devaluation and disempowerment, linked to an assumed non-contribution to the economy.

For older people who are also disabled, the experience of discrimination can be intensified.

A further ageist assumption of relevance to the notion of multiple oppressions is the asexual nature of old age. Whilst the myth that sexuality does not feature in old age persists, many sexually active older people will feel oppressed and alienated by the commonly held view that sexuality is only for younger people (Victor, 1994).

However, for gay and lesbian older people, this denial of sexuality can accentuate the 'heterosexism' to which they are already subject (GLC, 1985). Webb (1989) gives an example of this from a residential home for older people:

> accepting homosexuality was difficult enough if the person was young. If they were old, there was deliberate denial, even revulsion. Two women residents who loved and cared for one another were deliberately kept apart by staff. They were not allowed to share a room, even though this was their wish, and they were deliberately placed apart in the day room unable to move nearer because of their disabilities. (p. 20)

Clearly, then, there are many aspects, layers and dimensions to discrimination and oppression. Ageism is part of a complex web of oppressive forces which interact to produce a range of problematic situations for older people and, therefore, a range of challenges facing health and social welfare staff who work with older people.

Developing anti-ageist practice necessarily involves recognizing ageism in the context of discrimination and oppression more broadly:

> ageism is not simply another form of discrimination to be 'tagged on' to the more established issues of racism and sexism. Indeed, cleavages in society's structures do not occur in isolation but articulate with one another. Ageism is an important dimension of this complex matrix of multiple oppressions.
>
> Each of these oppressions has the effect of disempowering the people to whom it applies and thus stands in the way of citizenship. Where two or more of such oppressions combine, even greater barriers to citizenship are erected. (Thompson, 1992b, p. 39)

Practice focus 1.4

As part of her training course, Sandra interviewed a number of older people who attended the local day centre. She was undertaking a project on ageism and was therefore keen to talk to users of the centre about how they felt older people are treated in modern society. Sandra learned a great deal from this exercise but particularly from her discussions with Mrs Parwa about her experiences of oppression as a black woman. Mrs Parwa gave first-hand accounts of the discrimination she had encountered. This allowed Sandra to draw parallels between racism, sexism and ageism and to begin to understand some of the ways in which they interact and overlap.

Developing anti-ageist practice

Traditional approaches to working with older people have tended to neglect ageism and underestimate its significance in terms of its effects onthe lives of older people and its influence on health and social welfare practice. Developments in recent years have begun to highlight the significant role of ageism and the need to challenge and undermine its destructive effects.

One major implication of this is the need for staff to review their own practice – to reconsider how they go about their tasks and duties and re-evaluate their appropriateness in the light of what we now know about ageism and related forms of oppression. This is the challenge that now faces us – to develop ways of working with older people which build on existing strengths, but which also incorporate an anti-ageist perspective.

This challenge is a primary feature of the book, an attempt to combine old and new within an integrated framework. The 'old' involves reviewing established good practice developed over a considerable period of time. The 'new' involves constructing an approach to working with older people which:

- recognizes older people as an oppressed group;
- is sensitive to the three levels of ageism – personal, cultural and structural;
- seeks to challenge and undermine ageism;
- helps to empower older people and promote positive self-esteem.

This fourth point is particularly important, as one of the features of oppression is that it can become 'internalized' by the victims of that oppression. For example, black children exposed to racism often take on board a view of themselves as inferior (Ahmad, 1990). Similarly, it is not uncommon for older people to adopt ageist attitudes, to internalize negative views of themselves. Ageism presents older people as a nuisance, a social burden, and so elders can, within the context of an ageist society, perceive themselves as a nuisance or a burden. Marshall (1990) captures this point as follows:

> Ageism, like racism and sexism, is about prejudice against a section of the population. And prejudice is about ignorance, deprivation of power, stereotyping and so on. Ageism, like the others, is internalised by the victims who can share the stereotypes. (p. 88)

This issue of the internalization of oppression and the need for empowerment is of major significance and one which will recur in the chapters that follow. It raises a number of important implications for working with older people.

Developing anti-ageist practice is, as I have suggested, a major challenge. It will be a feature of each of the remaining chapters, as it is a central tenet of the book that good practice must be anti-ageist practice, insofar as to turn one's back on ageism is, at best, to allow it to continue, and, at worst, to add to the oppression. The final chapter will echo the main anti-ageist themes to emerge from the discussions in each of the chapters and seek to integrate them into the basis for developing the outline of a 'charter for anti-ageist practice'.

With this in mind, the focus now changes to a consideration of the ageing process – and, indeed, Chapter 2 seeks to develop an anti-ageist perspective on this process.

2 The ageing process

Introduction

The term 'the ageing process' is a commonly used one, but one that is rarely questioned or considered in any depth. In particular, there are two aspects of the concept of the 'ageing process' which rarely receive any attention:

1 It is commonly assumed that 'ageing' refers only to older people, that is, people in the latter stages of life. However, a closer analysis clearly reveals that ageing applies to everybody across the life-span, regardless of age. We are all getting older – the new-born baby as much as the elderly person.
2 The ageing process is generally seen as primarily a biological process. It is rarely recognized that it is a multidimensional process, incorporating a range of significant issues and influences.

Both these sets of issues are of particular significance. The first notion, that 'ageing' refers to old age, betrays a common attitude to growing older – a tendency to turn our backs on it, rather than face up to it. This is a significant issue in relation to the development of ageist attitudes and is a matter to be discussed below under the heading of 'The ontology of old age'.

The second point, that the ageing process has a number of dimensions, is a major feature of this chapter. I shall begin by considering the physical or biological dimension, explaining why it has taken the lion's share of attention in traditional studies of ageing, and summarizing the main changes which occur in later life. I shall then go on to explore the other major dimensions of the ageing process – psychological factors, the social construction and social context of old age, the politics and the ontology of ageing. The overall aim is to present a broad, overall picture of old age without falling foul of the common tendency to overemphasize the physical aspects.

The physical dimension

Descriptions of the ageing process often focus primarily, if not exclusively, on the physical or biological aspects of ageing – ageing is presented as what happens to a body, rather than to a person. This emphasis on the physical – especially on physical frailty – can be seen to be part and parcel of ageism. As Bytheway and Johnson (1990) comment:

> It is important to begin by identifying the essence of ageism. We would suggest that this is to be found in the consequences (social, economic, political, institutional, interpersonal and intrapersonal) of the interpretation of age as a basic source of biological variation between people and over the course of life.
> It is on the basis of biological differences, and in particular their visible manifestations, that people can be perceived to be of 'different kinds'. Just as it is biological variation which is employed to 'legitimate' distinctions on grounds of gender, disability and race, so it is the biology of the ageing process which is popularly perceived to justify beliefs about age. (p. 30)

This describes what is known as 'biological reductionism' – reducing a complex, multifaceted phenomenon to a simple matter of biology. Such reductionism, as we shall see below, serves a political function insofar as it distracts attention from wider social, political and economic matters, and thereby protects the status quo from undue questioning or challenge.

In exploring the physical dimension of old age, then, it is important to bear in mind the context in which such matters have normally been studied and discussed. We must see the biology of ageing as one part of a broader whole – one theme in a story, rather than the whole story.

In considering the biology of ageing, it is important to see the human body in terms of a number of ongoing processes – a dynamic development, rather than a static entity. Various processes of renewal or regeneration take place as a matter of course. Viewed in this context, the physical decline associated with old age can be seen as a slowing down or, in some respects, a cessation of this process. There are various theories which attempt to explain this (Bond *et al.*, 1993) but space does not permit a discussion of these here.

One common misunderstanding of this process is to regard old age as a disease process, a time of inevitable frailty and ailments. Victor (1991) argues that this negative stereotype supports the view of old age as a burden, and the increasing number of older people as a social problem:

> The imagery associated with later life is centred upon stereotypes of physical decline and the financial and social 'burden' of supporting older people . . . One area where this imagery of burden and decline is especially potent is that of ageing and health and the provision of health and social care services. Old age is inevitably associated with biological and physical decline. It is taken as quite natural that old age is a time of biological decline, which results in the entire population of older people being characterised by ill health and sickness. To be old is to be unhealthy. (p. 1)

Picton (1991) echoes this danger of seeing old age as a form of ill-health and argues that: 'While the part played by disease remains an important one, a pathological model of ageing is an inadequate basis for understanding the complex problems of old people' (p. 23).

Stuart-Hamilton (1994) draws a useful distinction between primary ageing, which refers to universal aspects of growing old (for example, the loss of hair pigmentation), and secondary ageing: 'changes which occur with greater frequency in old age, but are not a necessary accompaniment' (p. 7). Illness and physical disability would come into this category, but we must be careful not to equate increased likelihood of occurrence with inevitability, or even probability (Thompson, 1993).

Gross (1992) summarizes the work of Bee and Mitchell (1980) who provide an account of physical changes in old age under five headings, as follows:

- *Smaller*: Height tends to decrease due to the compression of connective tissues such as tendons, ligaments and muscles. A reduction in muscle mass and the size of organs, combined with a loss of calcium from the bones, also produces a reduction in body weight.
- *Slower*: Reaction times are slower due to the lower speed at which electrical nerve impulses travel to and from the brain. Liver and skin cells are renewed at a slower rate and fractures may also require a longer period to heal.
- *Weaker*: This manifests itself in a number of ways: bones become more brittle, muscle strength is reduced and the senses function at a reduced level of efficiency.
- *Lesser*: A reduction in the elasticity of the skin, eardrum, blood vessels and lens leads to wrinkling, reduced sensitivity to high frequency sounds, circulatory problems and a tendency to farsightedness, respectively.
- *Fewer*: Fewer taste buds can lead to reduced sensitivity to variations in food taste. There is also some thinning out of body hair and loss of nerves within the central nervous system.

Although this paints a fairly negative picture, it needs to be remembered that a reduction in capacity should not be equated with a lack of capacity – the changes described here are both relative and gradual.

A further important aspect of the physical dimension is that of sexuality. It is commonly, but mistakenly, assumed that sexuality ceases to apply in old age. As Gibson (1992) comments:

> the idea that 'old' people are, or should be, without sexual drive or capacity serves the function of jockeying them into a relatively powerless position in society. They are regarded as 'past it', and consequently not of fully adult status, to be pitied and patronized. (p. 16)

Practice focus 2.1

Tony was a very experienced nurse and had spent the last two years as a staff nurse on a geriatric ward. He had never associated any of his patients with sexuality. He was therefore totally taken aback when a female patient made a sexual remark to him. He could not believe his own eyes and ears when she winked at him and said she wished she were 50 years younger.

This myth of the asexual nature of old age is a pervasive one, reflecting the marginalization of older people – and the legitimation of such marginalization on biological grounds. This is an example of biological reductionism in which wider psychological and social factors are neglected, and the role and significance of the biological dimension are overstated. This is a point to which I shall return below.

In sum, then, the biological dimension of the ageing process involves a number of changes at different levels, but these changes need to be understood in terms of:

- a tendency for their negative effects to be exaggerated;
- the mistake of equating changes in old age with illness;
- the dangers of biological reductionism – failing to recognize that the physical dimension of ageing is only one amongst many.

The psychological dimension

The psychology of ageing is a broad-ranging subject and so we cannot do full justice to it in the space available here – it will be necessary to be selective. I shall focus in particular on providing an overview of two aspects – thinking and feeling or, to use the technical terms, cognition and affect.

Two important parts of cognition are intelligence and memory. Both of these are commonly assumed to decline in old age. Determining whether or not this is actually the case is not a straightforward matter. This is particularly so with regard to intelligence as there is considerable debate about what constitutes 'intelligence' (for example, in relation to IQ testing). One distinction which is of relevance to old age is that between crystallized intelligence and fluid intelligence:

> Raymond Cattell (1971) distinguished between fluid intelligence, the capacity for deductive reasoning and insight into complex relations, and crystallized intelligence, the ability to master and use acquired knowledge and skills. Fluid intelligence is assumed to be relatively independent of education and experience, whereas crystallized intelligence (defining words, solving arithmetic problems, or summarising the President's policy on the environment) depends heavily on culture and education.
>
> The research suggests that both kinds of intelligence increase throughout adolescence, but over the life span fluid ability slowly decreases and crystallized ability remains stable. (Wade and Tavris, 1993, p. 503)

There is some evidence, then, that one aspect of intelligence declines with age but the other does not. However, even though fluid intelligence may be seen to decline in general, it cannot be assumed that this would apply to all older people: 'It is important to note that the decline in fluid intelligence is not universal within an age group, and, some individuals may be largely immune to age changes' (Stuart-Hamilton, 1994, p.36).

There are similar complications with regard to the relationship between memory and old age. Wade and Tavris (1993) comment that: 'As people age, it takes them longer to retrieve names, dates and other facts. In this case the reason does seem to be their impaired perceptual-motor skills – their slower reaction times – not impaired memory itself' (p. 504). Hayes (1994) also makes the point that ageist stereotypes exaggerate the extent to which abilities decline in old age. The common assumption that old age is characterized by poor memory is therefore misleading.

Hayslip and Panek (1993) take this a step further and argue that ageist myths about memory create a vicious circle:

> The senility myth leads some older learners to lose self-confidence in their skills. For those who value 'brain power', it may even cause loss of self-respect. Other people may then expect less of them because they are forgetful. A vicious cycle has thus been established: further problems with learning or memory create more worry, and the worry contributes to more difficulties in concentration,

thereby interfering further with learning and memory skills. Rather than read a new book, try a crossword puzzle, or attend a lecture, these adults give up. 'I'm too old for that' may now be the silent message that our learner sends him or herself. Thus, learning difficulties or memory loss with increased age can become a self-fulfilling prophecy for some people. (p. 158)

This illustrates once again the dangers of biological reductionism – seeing memory as a physiological matter without paying due regard to the psychological and social issues involved.

The emotional or 'affective' dimension of ageing is one that has received far less attention than the cognitive aspects. Indeed, what little has been written tends to be largely negative in focus, for example in relation to depression.

One important point to recognize is that ageist stereotypes of older people preclude emotion, as if old age were a time without feelings. De Beauvoir (1977) echoes this when she discusses the myth of serenity, the distorted view of older people as calm and untroubled. Once again, we encounter an oversimplification of a complex matter – and, once again, it is at older people's expense.

Ageism is also significant in relation to emotion in terms of the 'internalization of oppression'. This is a term which refers to the process whereby the negative effects of discrimination and oppression are 'taken on board' by the person concerned. This internalization of oppression can manifest itself as low self-esteem and a negative self-image. That is, ageism not only affects older people at an objective level – in terms of a lack of respect, restricted life-chances and so on – it can also apply at a subjective level in terms of self-perception. For example, comments frequently heard in working with older people include: 'I don't like to be a nuisance' or 'Haven't you got other people who deserve your help more than I do?' These reflect the ageist notion that older people are a burden on society, a drain on the nation's resources – the oppression has become internalized.

The tendency for older people to experience lower self-esteem as a result of this process of internalization is a very important one, as it can have a major impact in terms of a lowering of confidence. Lower confidence can be very significant in terms of the ability to cope with adversity. For example, a person who is prone to falling may, if he or she loses confidence, become less mobile which, in turn, can reduce confidence further and thereby create a vicious circle of dependency – a process fuelled by ageist ideology which creates the expectation that old age is necessarily characterized by dependency.

Ironically, such dependency also raises emotional issues insofar as the need to depend on others can be experienced as emotionally painful and demeaning. This is especially so when staff involved in the caring process are less than sensitive to the emotional needs of the persons they are

---

Practice focus 2.2

Mr Davies was admitted to hospital after a fall. Whilst his physical injuries were not serious, the damage to his confidence was to prove very problematic. On returning home, he was very reluctant to leave his chair in case he fell again. This situation came to light when his home carer realized that he had not gone to bed, preferring to sleep in his armchair. When she discussed this with him, she soon understood that the fall had damaged his pride and his confidence. Although his body had been 'repaired' by medical attention, his confidence received no attention and remained very fragile.

---

working with. As Scrutton (1989) confirms, this can so easily have the effect of undermining dignity:

> When I started social work with older people, the failure of many otherwise caring people to understand the emotional impact of dependence was instantly striking. They had failed to think beyond the facts of the situation – that these people could no longer perform a task, and that as a caring person they would do it for them. Yet if, as carers, we can see no further than the physical need to care, we ignore the entire emotional significance of acts of caring on the dependent individual. An act which we intend as 'caring' can seem to be no more than an imposition on personal pride and dignity. (p. 150)

Such a neglect of the emotional dimension is both a reflection of, and contributor to, the tendency towards dehumanization, as discussed in Chapter 1.

The social construction of old age

In discussing the ageing process, we are, of course, discussing a process which is socially defined; that is, it is socially constructed:

> What is abundantly clear is that old age is a social construction – it is mediated by different social circumstances, including the consequences of class, race and gender inequality. Being defined as a social construction means that old age is not just a natural phenomenon, but one *endowed with social significance*. (Thompson and Thompson, 1993, p. 39, emphasis added)

Whilst ageing clearly has a biological dimension, it also has 'social significance' – the way old age (and indeed other stages of the life course) is experienced is heavily influenced by social factors, particularly social expectations of the role of older people in society.

In the same way that childhood can be seen to have been 'constructed' by changes in society following the invention of the printing press and the establishment of compulsory education (Musgrove, 1964; Postman, 1983), old age can also be seen to have been 'constructed' by the introduction of compulsory retirement. The development of the printing press introduced an emphasis on the need to learn to read. Prior to this, children were treated as 'small adults', not qualitatively different from the older generation. The fact that they could not read was not socially significant until the impact of the printing press.

A similar situation can be seen to apply to the way in which old age has come to be defined as a distinct life stage. With the advent of the Industrial Revolution, work opportunities became increasingly located at a distance from home, centralized in factories and other industrial units. Finkelstein (1981) has argued that this led to the exclusion of many disabled people from the workforce, as mobility limitations prevented them from maintaining their involvement in paid labour. This was a major step in constructing disabled people as a dependent group, reliant on others for their upkeep and separate from mainstream society. The same argument also applies to certain sections of the older population who could contribute to work at home but not in the more strictly regulated environment of the factory with its production schedules and complex division of labour.

However, Phillipson (1993a) warns against the danger of overemphasizing the role of industrialization in excluding older people from the workforce. He argues that issues of retirement have played a major role in this process. He outlines three factors which contributed to the significance of retirement:

> First, older people probably entered the new industries at a slower rate than younger workers. The reverse side of this is that they tended to be clustered in industries subject to economic decline. Secondly, retirement has to be seen in more global terms. For industrial capitalism, according to Graebner (1980), retirement provided a means of challenging security of tenure or jobs for life . . . Thirdly, as Graebner (1980) and Phillipson (1982) suggest, retirement has played an important role in periods of mass unemployment. (p. 146)

It is this, and related arguments, that lead Fennell *et al.* (1988) to argue that: 'old age can be viewed as a social construction formed out of demographic, economic and work processes' (p. 38). The economic dimension is one to which I shall return below.

The social construction of old age acts as a counterbalance to traditional medicalized conceptions of old age which take little or no account of the broader social context of ageing. In order to develop a better understanding of this social context, it is helpful to consider each of the main 'social divisions' as they relate to older people, building on the discussion of multiple oppressions in Chapter 1. I shall outline, in turn, the significance of class, race/ethnicity, gender and sexual orientation.

Class

Perhaps the most significant point to note in relation to class and old age is that reaching old age tends to have the effect of amplifying socioeconomic class differences. That is, differences between class groups become exaggerated by the social and economic changes brought about by retirement. This applies in two main ways, finance and lifestyle (the two are, of course, interrelated).

Finance relates primarily to preparation for old age in terms of pensions, savings and so on. Those who have greater earning power prior to retirement (for example, professionals) are more likely to:

- have a relatively high income at the point of retirement;
- have contributed to an occupational pension scheme;
- have accrued savings;
- own their own home and therefore not have to pay rent;
- have other sources of income, for example, from investments.

Those more accustomed to lower incomes, for example, manual workers, are far less likely to have access to such financial benefits. Some manual workers may be particularly disadvantaged, for example construction workers whose earning power decreases with age and whose reliance on short-term contracts seriously detracts from occupational pension eligibility. A professional worker, by contrast, would advance through an incremental scale and have the benefit of a relatively generous superannuation scheme.

Class differences are also quite noticeable in terms of what can broadly be described as lifestyles. These manifest themselves in terms of:

- leisure – for example, ownership of expensive equipment such as golf clubs or craftwork items;
- housing – differences in quality of housing can become very significant in old age, for example, heating and other facilities;
- health – the higher one's class position, the lower the incidence of illness (Townsend and Davidson, 1987);
- transport – reliance on public transport can limit mobility and so the ownership of a car, and the wherewithal to maintain and run it, can be very significant.

There are also class differences in terms of the transition from work to retirement. For example, manual workers face an abrupt transition when the compulsory retirement age is reached. Many professional workers, by contrast, have a more gradual transition through consultancy or other part-time involvement in work, thus facilitating a less traumatic withdrawal from the work environment and the social contacts and rewards this entails.

One's class background is therefore a significant feature of one's experience of the ageing process. It is an important factor which needs to be taken into consideration in working with people in the later stages of life. To ignore this aspect of a person's experience is yet another example of the insidious process of dehumanization.

Race/ethnicity

Race is a term which has strong biological connotations, but this is misleading:

> Race is not a biological category, it is a process – a social and political process whereby ethnic differences are translated into pseudo-biological racial deficits. In this way the seeds of racism are sown. Discrimination against black and ethnic minority peoples is legitimated on the basis of assumed racial inferiority. (Thompson, 1993, p. 59)

Thus, it is important to acknowledge that good practice in working with older people needs to be:

- *Ethnically sensitive*: It must take account of people's varying cultural needs, including diet, dress, festivals and other religious observances.
- *Anti-racist*: Recognizing cultural differences is the first step but we also need to recognize that such differences often lead to discrimination and oppression on racial grounds. Good practice therefore involves challenging and undermining racism.

Perhaps the biggest barrier to achieving these two goals is the not uncommon attitude of 'we treat everybody the same'. It is often mistakenly assumed that treating everybody the same is a way of ensuring equality (the 'colour-blind' approach). However, this fails to address two key issues:

1   Differing cultural needs are overlooked and this can be a profoundly alienating and oppressive experience. Equality involves recognizing and respecting difference.

2   If people start from a position of inequality and disadvantage, 'treating everybody the same' will reinforce or even accentuate such inequality. Equality is something we have to work towards, rather than take for granted.

Practice focus 2.3

Indira Begum was admitted to a nursing home when her family no longer felt able to look after her. At first, she seemed to settle well but soon became very withdrawn and depressed. Her relatives were very impressed with the standard of nursing care in the home and therefore made no connection between the nursing care provided and Indira's deteriorating condition. However, on one particular visit Indira's daughter noticed an uneaten meal on a tray next to her mother's bed. She was surprised and disappointed to find the meal consisted of traditional western fare, wholly unlike the type of food her mother was accustomed to eating. Further investigation revealed that no allowance had been made for her mother's cultural preferences with regard to food or other aspects of daily living. A picture therefore began to form – a distressing picture in which Indira felt marginalized, alienated and, consequently, devalued.

When the issue was raised with the officer in charge, her response was simple and straightforward. She believed in treating everybody the same – in order to avoid drawing attention to people's differences. Despite the 'good intentions' underlying this 'colour-blind' approach, the actual outcome was a negative and discriminatory one. Despite nursing standards being high in other respects, this lack of sensitivity to ethnic needs had produced a racist outcome (Thompson, 1995b).

These issues of ethnically sensitive and anti-racist practice apply across the board in working with people, regardless of their age. There are, however, issues of race and ethnicity that apply specifically to old age.

One very important point to recognize is that the class differentials discussed earlier tend to be intensified and amplified for older people from ethnic minorities. As Biggs (1993) comments:

> A history of migration and settlement, plus the status of 'replacement labour' increases the difficulties facing black elders (Patel, 1990), most of whom are working class. The 'migrant' cohort of elders experienced physically demanding work rejected by the existing population, resulting in more unemployment in times of scarcity, plus greater disability over time, whilst reducing the length of national insurance contributions that determine entitlement. (p. 90)

This illustrates the ways in which the odds can be stacked against older people from ethnic minorities as a result of a combination of historical and social factors.

These are structural issues, located at the 'S' level within the PCS framework. But there are also cultural issues to consider (the 'C' level), particularly in relation to stereotypes, distorted views of black elders.

There are two stereotypical comments which have tended to become recurring themes. The first of these is encapsulated in the saying: 'They look after their own'. This is a reference to the false assumption that members of ethnic minorities have extended families to rely upon for support, and therefore do not require services. This is, of course, an overgeneralization. Many cultures do have a strong tradition of supportive extended families, but this is not to say that all black cultures do.

Sometimes, the term 'black culture' is used, as if there were only one. Clearly this is a gross oversimplification of a complex situation involving a vast range of cultures with varying degrees, types and styles of family support. In addition, there are two further factors which complicate the matter:

1   For many black elders, their extended family may not be living in the same country and cannot therefore provide direct support.
2   Even where there is a supportive extended family, there may be reasons why this cannot be taken on board – family conflicts, for example. Cultural norms do not apply to every individual in every case.

Unfortunately, the problems associated with the notion of 'They look after their own' are not always appreciated, and it can be used, wittingly or otherwise, for not offering ethnically sensitive practice.

The second false assumption derives from the notion that: 'They do not mix'. This is based on the mistaken view that a wish to safeguard one's own culture and heritage amounts to a desire not to mix with people of other cultures. But the notion of 'They do not mix' is not simply a 'mistake', it is also a powerful legitimation of racial separatism. That is, this apparently innocent saying undermines the concept of a multicultural society, and thereby subtly reinforces the idea of white superiority. Also, it once again provides an excuse for not providing ethnically sensitive services, or a false explanation of the low take-up rate of services (Blakemore and Boneham, 1994).

In summary, then, the experience of old age for members of ethnic minorities is significantly different from that of their white counterparts. This is for two main reasons:

1   *Ethnicity*: Cultural norms and differences are frequently ignored, disregarded or devalued.

2 *Race*: Black elders also encounter racism at three different levels: personal prejudice from staff or other service users (Ahmad-Aziz *et al.*, 1992); a discriminatory culture as evidenced by derogatory stereotypes; and institutional or structural racism as a result of organizations, and society at large, failing to take adequate account of the needs of older people from ethnic minorities.

Gender

Gender is a significant aspect of old age, if for no other reason than the fact that women outnumber men to a major extent. There are, of course, many other ways in which gender plays a key role in the process of ageing.

One issue worthy of note is the 'myth of continuity' for women. That is, it is commonly assumed that, while men experience a potentially traumatic transition from work to retirement, women enjoy a degree of continuity. Biggs (1993) refers to Phillipson's (1982) rejection of this myth:

> Phillipson (1982) takes issue with the view that women are relatively unaffected by formal working life, pointing to the large numbers of women in poorer paid, less skilled and auxiliary occupations. Much of this work fails to provide an adequate income in retirement, reducing opportunities for leisure and independence. Even so, semi-skilled women workers have been found to be more resistant to retirement than men, as they gave greater priority to social ties formed within the workplace. (p. 95)

A high proportion of women therefore face the same transition from work to retirement that men do, with a similar range of potential problems. This is often seen as less demanding for women as they maintain the role of 'home-maker' and therefore have more stability and continuity than their male counterparts. However, Bernard and Meade (1993a) challenge the validity of this argument:

> Until recently, most of the literature on retirement concentrated on the experience of men. Retirement, the argument went, was of prime importance to men because it marked a fundamental status change, that from worker to non-worker, and involved a substantial period of adjustment to one's altered circumstances. Women, on the other hand, even if they had been in paid employment, would find the retirement transition easier largely because of the 'other roles' (the women's work!) they were still likely to be engaged in, and which they could readily substitute for work. Maxine Szinovacz (1982) counters this, arguing first, that there is little evidence that discontinuity in employment correlates with a lack of commitment that might make for an easier adjustment to retirement, and second, that domestic tasks are unlikely to provide an effective substitute for the personal social and material rewards of paid employment. (p. 149)

Clearly, then, simplistic uncritical assumptions about women's experience of old age and retirement are very much to be avoided.

A further aspect of the relationship between gender and old age is that of caring. In patriarchal societies, caring is traditionally seen as a role for women, and this is indeed the case in respect of caring for older people where the vast majority of carers are in fact women. Chapter 7 addresses the question of carers, and so I shall return to this issue and discuss it in more detail at that point.

Old age has different sets of implication for men and women. For women, both ageism and sexism have to be faced. Hughes and Mtezuka (1992) comment on two particular aspects of this:

> Ageism and sexism are connected in two ways. First, the impact of ageing on women has implications for the extent to which old women can conform to the image of womanhood propagated by sexism. A woman not only loses the physical attractiveness ascribed to the ideal woman, but also the prescribed social roles of caring for the family. Indeed, she may need care herself and, as the carer becomes the cared-for, a role reversal underlines the failure of the older woman to conform to the stereotype of womanhood. Thus, passage into old age increases the potential for dissonance with social norms of womanhood and femininity.
>
> Second, an old woman evokes primeval images of women as mystics and witches, derived from woman's proximity to (and men's alienation from) the processes of nature. (p. 223)

Sexism is also an issue for men in old age. Men's roles in patriarchal societies are strongly influenced by rigid notions of masculinity which can be seen as a mixed blessing. That is, while men gain power and privilege from sexism, they also incur costs in terms of certain behaviours being seen as 'unmanly' (Thompson, 1995a). For example, men are discouraged from expressing grief and sadness – 'big boys don't cry'. This is particularly apparent when a significant loss is experienced and traditional masculinity acts as a barrier to effective grieving (Thompson, 1994b). This is an important issue with regard to old age for, as I shall argue below, the later stages of life are characterized by loss. In this respect, a traditional masculine upbringing can leave men ill-equipped to cope with the losses associated with old age.

Gender, then, is another example of the social dimension of the ageing process, another step away from the traditional overemphasis on the biological dimension of ageing.

Sexual orientation

The point was made in Chapter 1 that implicit within ageism is the assumption that older people are non-sexual beings – and, for gay and lesbian older people, their sexuality is doubly denied. The sexual orientation of an individual is therefore a further important element in the social dimension of ageing.

Very relevant to this is the 'cohort effect'. This refers to the fact that those people who are old today (the current cohort) will have certain things in common, for example, having lived through the 1930s depression and the Second World War. That is, they have much in common which is not related to being old *per se*, but to being old at this particular point in history.

Attitudes to homosexuality are a good example of the cohort effect. Today's generation of older people will have been brought up in times when a far more punitive and disapproving attitude towards homosexuality was firmly established as the norm:

> it is homosexual men in the older generation who have been through most traumatic experiences during a long period of their lives when their sexual expression was forbidden under the criminal law. They form a special group who are different in many ways from the homosexual men in younger generations. (Gibson, 1992, p. 151)

There is, therefore, something of a 'generation gap' with regard to homosexuality, with older people now living in a less oppressive age, but still with the internalized oppression of their earlier years affecting their thoughts, feelings and actions. For older gay men in particular, old age can be seen as a time characterized by conflicting values and expectations.

Gibson (1992) also comments on the issue of lesbianism in old age and relates this to the predominance of women in later life:

> There is now quite a body of contemporary literature discussing lesbianism, much of it being written by feminists who regard it as a natural alternative for those who do not wish to be involved sexually with men. As there is a great shortage of available men in the later decades of life, it would seem that there is a reasonable case for single women forming lesbian associations with one another, even though they have been exclusively heterosexual in their younger years. (p. 234)

How realistic this is for the majority of older women remains to be seen, given the complex interaction of social and emotional factors which impinge on sexuality.

The interrelationships of ageing and sexual orientation form an under-researched area and one about which we have much to learn. We are, however, beginning to learn more about this aspect of old age, as Hayslip and Panek (1993) confirm:

In a recent series of studies, we have learned a great deal about how gays and lesbians adjust to aging. Adelman (1990) found that men who were more satisfied with being gay adjusted better to growing old. They expressed higher life satisfaction, had more self-esteem, and reported few psychosomatic problems . . . Bennett and Thompson (1990) found that homosexual men may, in some cases, experience 'accelerated aging', that is, they are considered old at an earlier age than their heterosexual counterparts. (p. 256)

If we are to offer sensitive services which take account of sexual orientation as an important part of a person's life, then clearly, we have a long way to go in understanding what the important issues are and how they should best be handled. A necessary first step in this direction, of course, is to challenge the ageist myth that presents old age as an asexual period in a person's life.

The political dimension

In discussing the social dimension of ageing, it was noted that the social construction of old age is premised, in part at least, on economic factors relating to labour supply and demand. This reflects a 'political economy' approach to understanding the ageing process, as developed by writers such as Phillipson (1982), Walker (1986) and Townsend (1986). It involves recognizing that:

Older people are seen as marginal to the labour market and are therefore assigned a lower status due to the emphasis on measuring social value in terms of one's contribution to the production of wealth. Old age therefore needs to be understood in economic and political terms. (Thompson, 1993, p. 94)

Ageing is therefore not without its political implications. As we progress through the life course, our position in terms of power, status and rights alters according to our age group. Children have fewer rights, lower status and less power than adults (Stainton Rogers and Stainton Rogers, 1992). As we reach adulthood, our position is strengthened considerably, both in a legal sense (voting rights, for example) and in a sociological sense (greater independence and life-chances). However, on reaching old age, a decline in one's social position tends to occur. Older people enter what Midwinter (1990) calls 'postadulthood', a period of lesser citizenship in which rights are undermined by ageism:

Citizenship is strongly associated with the concept of 'adulthood'. Children are not generally seen as having the same rights as adults and older people are often treated as though they have 'passed through' adulthood and thus lost full rights and dignity. (Thompson, 1992b, p. 31)

As mentioned earlier, this is often reflected in the way Social Services Departments are structured with the common organizational pattern of a division of services into three categories or service areas: children and families; adult services; and elderly services, thereby implying that elderly people are not adults.

Power and rights are therefore negatively associated with old age – the latter stages of life are characterized by a decline in citizenship. It is, of course, no coincidence that this should be the case. As we have seen, old age is 'socially constructed', a period within the life course defined by reference to economic factors in terms of labour and production. Walker (1991) makes the point quite forcefully:

> The increasing dependency of elderly people in Britain has been socially engineered in order to remove older workers from the labour force. At the heart of this social change has been the narrow financial goals of capitalism, and particularly its constant desire to increase profitability. In this interest mass superannuation has been managed through the retirement, early retirement and unemployment of older workers. Age-restrictive social policies have been used by the state both to exclude older workers from the labour force and to legitimate that exclusion through retirement. Retirement pensions are one of the means by which capitalism is able to enforce changes aimed at reconstituting the workforce. This changing social relationship between age and the labour market has formed the basis for a more general spread of dependency among the elderly. (p. 54)

This process of older people being excluded from the labour market, and society more generally, is further exemplified by 'disengagement theory' (Cumming and Henry, 1961) which presents a withdrawal from social and political life as a 'natural' part of the life course. According to this theory, a gradual withdrawal or 'phasing out' from certain social roles or aspects of society takes place, thus ensuring that society has the opportunity to adjust to the loss of the individual without undue disruption. This is presented as an inevitable and healthy part of old age – a view which has been strongly challenged:

> As a general sociological theory, in which ageing was seen as a normal and necessary process of disengagement whereby the individual withdrew from the major roles of life whilst society concomitantly ceased to depend on the individual for the performance of those roles, disengagement theory aroused immediate controversy . . . objections to the theory have been considerable. It was pointed out that social disengagement is not universal. When it did occur it was not related to age as such but to various losses and stresses connected with age, such as bereavement, retirement or ill health. Most importantly, some studies indicated that those who did not disengage but remained active and socially integrated had a greater degree of life satisfaction than those who did disengage. (Coleman, 1993, pp. 84–5)

Disengagement theory can therefore be seen as a 'legitimation' – that is, an implicit justification – of older people being disenfranchised, deprived to a greater or lesser extent of their full status as citizens. Again, we encounter the political dimension of old age in the form of undermining the rights, power and status of older people – in short, ageism.

The ontology of old age

Ontology is the study of being: 'Ontology raises fundamental questions about meaning, value and purpose. It is therefore of major significance in relation to issues of life, death, grief and loss' (Thompson, 1994b, p. 1). By the same token, ontology is also significant in relation to old age, as old age is, by definition, the final stage of life.

In this respect, old age can be seen as a time of life which has a particular ontological significance and relevance. In fact, the ontological question of facing up to death is one that applies throughout the life course, as death is an ever-present possibility throughout life. The notion that older people are 'closer to death' is therefore not as simple as it may first seem, as de Beauvoir (1977) argues:

> The truth of the matter is that the idea of death's coming closer is mistaken. Death is neither near nor far: it is not. Over all living beings, whatever their age, there hangs an inescapable exterior fate: in no case is there a set moment at which this fate will strike. The old man knows that he will die 'soon': the fatality is as present at seventy as it is at eighty, and the word 'soon' remains as vague at eighty as it was at seventy. It is not correct to speak of a relationship with death: the fact is that the old man, like all other men, has a relationship with life and with nothing else. (p. 492)

It is important, then, if we are not to succumb to the negativism of ageism, that old age is seen as a time of life, not of death. Death is intertwined with life throughout the life course and is therefore not an issue specific to old age. However, what is specific to old age is the greater opportunity to come to terms with the finite nature of human existence and the inevitability of death. The reason for this is that old age is a time of life characterized by loss, a time in which our mortality is emphasized by the likely experience of multiple losses, including the following:

- dignity and respect – as a result of ageism;
- the death of friends and contemporaries;
- the death of other important figures in one's life, for example singers, film stars, writers;
- functional ability, for example through arthritis;

- social roles, power and influence.

The experience of loss is, of course, not uniform and considerable variation is to be expected. The encounter with loss, though (particularly multiple losses), does have the effect of raising ontological questions – the pain of loss emphasizes our vulnerability and human frailty. As Morgan (1993) comments:

> The first conclusion one can draw about human spirituality is that the human quest is a quest for meaning. We are not an instinctual animal. We are the only animal that has to decide from moment to moment, who am I? What do I have to do?
> It is in precisely the confrontation with death and loss that we become fully aware of the human situation. We, and everyone we love, will die. In spite of our uniqueness, we are still radically contingent and will someday cease to be. (p. 5)

Old age, then, presents us with an existential challenge. And, as Biggs (1993) implies, ageism acts as a barrier to achieving success by attaching more importance to the life tasks facing younger people:

> existential priorities, that is to say the tasks of personal renewal and the creation of meaning, differ with age. This is most notable between earlier and later periods of life . . . the legitimacy afforded these priorities, or projects, is given differential value, with those of relative youth eclipsing those of later life. (p. ix)

Matters of death and dying are also paid more attention when they relate to younger people. Moss and Moss (1993) point out that there is a considerable literature on sudden death and the death of children, whilst the issues of death in old age remain under-researched. Gerontology has remained relatively silent on the subject of death and dying (Sidell, 1993).

Clearly, then, the ontological dimension of old age is both an important one and a relatively neglected one. As we pass through the final stages of life, questions of meaning and purpose take on an extra significance and so it becomes necessary for us to acknowledge the ontological dimension of the ageing process as a basic feature of the experience of old age. It is therefore essential that we recognize that to continue to neglect its significance could prove very costly in terms of developing an approach to working with older people premised on dignity and empowerment.

Conclusion

Growing old is a 'natural' process in that it is an inevitable movement from birth, through the life course, to death. It is also 'natural' in the sense that

---

Practice focus 2.4

Carol was a social worker who enjoyed working with older people. However, one thing she did not relish was arranging respite care. This was because she was required to fill in a form which included details of preferences for funeral arrangements (in case of death whilst in respite care). Carol felt extremely uncomfortable raising the issue. On one particular occasion she was quite apologetic for introducing the subject. She was then very surprised indeed at the response she received, namely a hearty laugh and the comment: 'Here I am, three times your age, and yet you're the one who's frightened to talk about death!' Carol realized that her professional training had left her feeling ill-equipped to deal with issues of death and dying.

---

there is a distinct biological dimension. However, as we have seen, it is misleading to follow the traditional path of overemphasizing the biological basis of ageing at the expense of the various other dimensions – especially as biological explanations are used as a means of legitimating ageism (Bytheway and Johnson, 1990).

In order to avoid adopting too narrow a perspective, it is important to bear in mind the multidimensional nature of the ageing process, thereby bringing into the picture a number of other aspects:

- the psychological;
- the social;
- the political;
- the ontological.

In developing anti-ageist practice, the focus must therefore be on the broader picture – as each of these aspects has implications for older people's lives – rather than too narrowly attuned to the biological dimension. In short, to ignore the biological aspect is foolish, to concentrate almost exclusively upon it is dangerous.

3   The policy context

Introduction

Working with older people is not an activity that occurs in a vacuum. We need to understand day-to-day practice in relation to the broader context of law and policy. We need to see how practice fits into the broader picture of the legal framework and the policy base. This chapter therefore seeks to sketch out some of the key elements of the policy context.

The two words which have a central role to play are 'law' and 'policy', and each of these is relevant in two senses. The law is used both to restrict and to enable. The restrictive aspect of the law relates to the ways in which the law forbids certain courses of action – they are deemed to be 'illegal'. That is, the law plays a significant part in determining what is and what is not permissible. For example, some forms of elder abuse are liable to prosecution under the law.

The law can also be enabling by giving staff the power to undertake certain courses of action. For example, the National Health Service (NHS) and Community Care Act 1990 empowers staff to undertake an assessment of social and health care needs and, where possible, provide or arrange the services to meet those needs.

The two ways in which policy is relevant are at the broader, macro level, and the narrower, micro level. At a macro level, policy refers to social policy, the body of government laws, regulations, guidelines and codes of practice which provide the context and framework for health and social welfare practice. In this way, law and policy overlap – the law is part of the broader backcloth of social policy (Hill, 1988).

Policy at the micro level refers to the specific policies of particular organizations, for example, the policy of a health service trust with regard to the provision of certain forms of treatment. Even at this level, though, law and policy are intertwined insofar as such policies have to be consistent with the law, and may have their roots in a particular legal provision or requirement.

The policy context, then, with its close links with the law, is a significant influence on the nature and scope of practice. This chapter therefore seeks to provide an overview of the main elements of social policy relating to older people, linking these, as far as possible, to specific pieces of legislation. I shall begin with a brief outline of the policy process, the process by which something is identified as a social problem and a policy response to it is constructed and implemented.

The policy process

The first stage in the development of a social policy is generally that of problem definition. That is, the policy process begins with something being defined as a problem. This is an important point as it confirms that social problems are socially constructed (Hulley and Clarke, 1991). That is, a social problem is something that society (or, more specifically, powerful individuals, groups and institutions within society) defines as problematic. As Samson (1994) comments:

> Social problems, as Edelman (1987) has argued, are categories of events that are invented, dropped and reinvented according to changing confluences of political and material interests . . . A social problem, then, is not a fixed property of a society, but an invention of a particular branch of the state which is put forward in order to justify a particular 'solution'. (p. 80)

The media have an important part to play in defining social problems as they reflect, amplify and channel public concern about social ills. At the end of the day, however, it is the Government that develops social policies. The Government's response may be to set up a working party or Royal Commission. This involves setting up a group of respected individuals to investigate the problem and to produce a report which proposes a solution or a set of measures to deal with the issues identified. A good example of this is the Griffiths Report on community care (Griffiths, 1988) which led to the National Health Service (NHS) and Community Care Act 1990.

Such reports may then become the basis of a Government 'white paper' which, in effect, is a proposal for legislation. Commonly, an amended version of the white paper becomes a 'Bill' – legislation in draft form. For a Bill to become an Act of Parliament, it has to be 'read' in either the House of Commons or the House of Lords, to begin with. Here, it has its 'First Reading'. This is basically a formal announcement and is quickly followed by the 'Second Reading', at which point the proposals are debated:

The Bill goes to a Standing Committee for detailed consideration, clause by clause . . . The Report stage then follows, when the amendments made in committee are considered and perhaps altered, but if further detailed amendments are sought, the Bill has to be returned to the Committee . . . Finally, the Bill is debated once more in general terms, with only verbal amendments allowed, and is given a Third Reading. The Bill then passes to the other House, where the process is repeated. (Punnett, 1976, p. 227)

But, even then, the process is not complete. The Bill has to receive Royal Assent before it becomes law.

This, then, is a detailed and thorough process which involves looking closely at the policy implications of the proposed Act of Parliament. Some may feel reassured, then, that the needs of vulnerable older people are likely to be well catered for. However, this optimistic view fails to take account of structural factors relating to the role of power in the policy process.

A factor not often appreciated is that, at each stage of the policy process, decision-making is dominated by people in positions of power – members of dominant groups in society. That is, decisions relating to relatively powerless people are made predominantly by white, able-bodied males. There is, therefore, an inherent bias in the policy process. Williams (1989) goes a step further by arguing that the whole of social policy marginalizes oppressed groups:

In general, 'race' and gender are issues that have been neglected or marginalized in the discipline of social policy, particularly in terms of a failure to, first, acknowledge the experiences and struggles of women and of Black people over welfare provision; secondly, to account for racism and sexism in the provision of state welfare; thirdly, to give recognition to work which does analyse the relationship between the welfare state and the oppressions of women and of Black people (and, historically, other racialized groups like the Irish and Jews); and fourthly, to work out a progressive welfare strategy which incorporates the needs and demands which emerge from such strategies and analyses. (p. xi)

It is therefore important that we should not adopt a naive attitude that sees health and welfare in entirely benevolent terms. The situation is a complex one in which major power interests have a part to play – it is not simply a matter of compassionate philanthropy. Braye and Preston-Shoot (1992) make a similar point in relation to the law:

The law preserves the status quo within the power structures of society. Whilst predicated upon the rhetoric of freedom, justice and equality, the law colludes with inequalities between women and men, black people and white people, people with disabilities and able-bodied, young and old . . . Class, gender and racial biases in the judiciary and in the law-making machinery of Parliament are matched by complementary over-representation of disadvantaged and less powerful groups in the statistics of those selected for compulsory intervention by the state. (p. 16)

In considering the policy context of working with older people, it is therefore important to recognize the complex nature of the web of factors that underpin law and policy, not least the significance of power relations in influencing the direction and impact of policy. That is, we need to bear in mind that the policy context is not simply a set of neutral rules and expectations – it is a reflection of the structure of society. Therefore, an uninformed and uncritical approach to law and policy can be fraught with difficulties in terms of reinforcing inequalities, discrimination and oppression. Once again, an anti-discriminatory approach is necessary in order to develop forms of practice which challenge ageism and other forms of oppression.

The Welfare State

Another important set of issues with regard to the policy context of working with older people relates to the Welfare State. *The Encyclopaedia Britannica* defines the Welfare State as a:

> concept of government in which the state plays a key role in the protection and promotion of the economic and social well-being of its citizens. It is based on the principles of equality of opportunity, equitable distribution of wealth, and public responsibility for those unable to avail themselves of the minimal provisions for a good life. The general term may cover a variety of forms of economic organization. (12: 569)

There is considerable debate over what can be termed the official beginning of the Welfare State in Britain, but changes in the 1940s certainly played a major role in shaping the modern Welfare State. In particular, three 'pillars' of the Welfare State dating back to the 1940s can be identified, namely the Education Act 1944, the National Health Service Act 1946 and the National Assistance Act 1948. The first of these does not have a direct bearing on services for older people, although it is important to note that it was this Act which introduced compulsory education for all children. Consequently, today's 'cohort' of older people will vary considerably in terms of their early life educational experiences. The other two 'pillars' are discussed later in this chapter, along with other major pieces of social policy legislation.

In addition to the three pillars, an important aspect of the Welfare State has been the development of 'social' housing. This refers to the recognition that housing should not simply be left to the private market, but should, rather, be supported by State intervention. This applies in terms of:

- provision of local authority housing;
- government financial support for housing associations;
- housing benefits;
- grant aid for repairs of certain properties;
- mortgage tax relief for house buyers.

With regard to older people, the most significant aspect of housing policy is the development of 'sheltered accommodation' – usually purpose-built housing units with alarm systems to summon help and/or warden supervision. According to Tinker (1992, p. 121), some 5 per cent of older people live in sheltered accommodation.

Since 1979, however, the Welfare State has undergone considerable change due to what has become known as the 'breakdown of consensus' following the election of a Conservative Government with strong views on the provision of health and welfare services (Johnson, 1990). Prior to this time, there had been a broad consensus across the main political parties with regard to welfare. Differences between Conservative and Labour were mainly differences of emphasis, rather than major disagreements over policy.

However, the development of Thatcherism as a major political force in Britain led to a radical critique of the Welfare State based on a number of premises:

- the aim of 'rolling back the State' in order to reduce the role of government and cut back on public expenditure;
- to encourage a greater reliance on the market as a regulator of supply and demand;
- to eliminate the perceived tendency for the Welfare State to encourage dependency and thereby sap initiative and enterprise;
- to make the Welfare State more cost-effective by targeting services more effectively.

Consequently, a number of services previously provided by the State are now to be found in the private and voluntary sectors; market consider-ations are much more to the fore than was previously the case; many benefits and services are far less accessible than before; and there is a greater emphasis on costs and greater control over expenditure.

These are important changes and will be particularly significant in relation to the discussion below of community care. These changes are also significant insofar as they underline the relationship between policy and power, policy being clearly and firmly rooted in politics.

Perhaps one of the premises of Thatcherism that can be readily and easily challenged is the notion of the 'nanny' State, the idea that the provision of benefits and services makes people dependent and reluctant to fend for themselves. Whilst this is arguably a dubious premise in respect of the Welfare State as a whole, its applicability with regard to older people is clearly unfounded, for the following reasons:

- Older people are often reluctant to accept help because they do not wish to be seen as a burden or nuisance (an example of internalized ageist oppression – see Chapter 4).
- The current generation of older people were brought up in the days of the workhouse, and many still associate State services with the fear, shame and stigma of the workhouse.
- Many older people would not be able to survive without the support and services they receive.
- Much of the Welfare State provision intended to support older people is geared towards aiding carers in their role. Without the immense efforts of informal carers, the statutory, voluntary and commercial sectors would certainly be in no position to cope with the demands (Johnson, 1987).

Practice focus 3.1

Mrs Linton lived alone and had no relatives in the area. Her neighbour, Mrs Jarvis, was becoming increasingly concerned about her and often contacted Social Services, the GP and the health visitor. However, Mrs Linton remained adamant that she did not need anyone's help and refused to receive services of any kind. At first, Mrs Jarvis felt that Mrs Linton should be forced to receive help, for her own good. Eventually she came to accept that her elderly neighbour had the right to refuse services and, like many older people, chose to exercise that right.

The notion that the Welfare State creates dependency, at a general level, for older people is clearly a false one. However, there is one danger we need to recognize – in their efforts to be caring and supportive, staff may inhibit independence. That is, whilst there is nothing intrinsically dependency-creating about providing services, the way in which they are delivered may prove counterproductive. This is a point to which we shall return in Chapter 5.

Health and welfare services for older people need to be understood in the context of the Welfare State, but a Welfare State that has changed considerably in recent years and which is continuing to change. In order to maintain an adequate understanding of the policy context of working with older people, we must therefore keep abreast of changes and developments in this important area of policy and politics.

The National Health Service Act 1946

In 1942 the Beveridge Report was published – a report that led to major and significant changes not only in social policy, but also in social life more broadly (Beveridge, 1942). Beveridge identified what he referred to as the 'five giant evils': want, disease, ignorance, squalor and idleness, and these correspond, respectively, to the policy areas of income maintenance, health, education, housing and employment.

The main topic of the report was the provision of social security – cash benefits for those unable to earn a living through employment. However, what also emerged from the report was the need for a national system of health care and related services. This point of view received considerable public support, and so it was not surprising that the coalition government of the time took the idea very seriously.

One major consequence of this was the development and implementation of the National Health Service Act 1946. As the name implies, this Act led to the introduction of the National Health Service, based on a number of key principles, including:

- Health care should be available for all people, free of charge at the point of delivery. That is, poverty should not act as a barrier to receiving health services.
- Increased national health should lead, in due course, to lower expenditure on health care.
- Health is a national or collective responsibility as well as an individual one.

It is significant that, in recent years, the first principle has been undermined to a certain extent by: large rises in prescription charges; a reduction in NHS dental services; some services not being available to people over a certain age, and so on. The second principle proved to be a false assumption. Increased access to health care led to a steadily increasing demand for services, rather than a reduction. Consequently, the NHS has, over the decades, experienced problems with escalating costs and the challenge of responding to seemingly infinite demand with finite resources. This has brought about a strong emphasis on efficiency and cost-effectiveness.

This emphasis is also significant in relation to the third principle as we have seen a movement away from collective responsibility towards needs being met only within certain budgetary limitations. Due, in no small part, to ageism, older people have fared very badly in this respect, bearing the brunt of cutbacks and 'streamlining'. Furthermore, Henwood (1993) comments that:

> within the National Health Service, it has been acute and curative services which have been developed, despite attempts to shift the balance towards preventive and caring services directed at chronic conditions. Older people are not the only group to be disadvantaged by such trends. The phrase 'Cinderella Services' was coined to describe the relative paucity of care for the mentally ill, people with learning difficulties and people with physical disabilities as well as elderly people. These groups share the characteristics of having long-term and chronic needs. Because of the scale of increase in the older population, however, it is the very old and frail who are seen to represent the greatest challenge to the health and community care services. (pp. 112–13)

The development of a national health service, as opposed to a 'national illness service', has therefore been held back. Although professional groups recognize and stress the importance of health education, promotion and preventative work, the primary focus remains clearly on attempts to 'cure'.

It should be clear, then, that the basic principles underlying the development of the National Health Service have come under considerable threat, particularly with regard to the needs of older people, and continue to be vulnerable.

The National Assistance Act 1948

This was a major piece of legislation that encompassed a wide range of issues. For present purposes, I shall concentrate on three particular areas: national assistance, Part III accommodation, and compulsory removal from home.

National assistance was the term used to describe financial benefits for those not covered by national insurance, payments to be made at subsistence level to act as a safety net for those not able to provide for themselves by other means. The term 'social security' was later used as a replacement for the notion of national assistance, and this mainly takes the form of income support. Older people may be able to claim income support to supplement their pension. Also, as Tinker (1992) comments, income support 'may also be a passport to other benefits such as free dental treatment, grants for insulation, and grants from the social fund' (p. 59). This is a complex and detailed area, and older people often do not receive the benefits to which they are entitled, a point to which I shall return in Chapter 5 when the issue of welfare benefits advice and advocacy is discussed.

'Part III' is a term commonly used to refer to residential accommodation provided for older people, but is not always recognized as a reference to Part III of the National Assistance Act 1948. Part III of the Act places a duty on local authorities to provide accommodation for those in need of care and attention by reason of age, illness, disability or other such circumstances. Traditionally, the provision of such accommodation, assessment for admission, and related matters, have been a major feature of social work with older people. However, as we shall see below, the NHS and Community Care Act 1990 has produced a major change of emphasis with regard to the provision and use of residential accommodation.

The National Assistance Act 1948 also introduced the possibility of older people being removed from home on a compulsory basis in certain circumstances. As Fishwick (1992, p. 121) comments:

> The National Assistance Act 1948 provides for the compulsory removal from home to a hospital or other suitable place of certain persons for whom it is necessary to secure care and attention. Section 47 of the Act applies to persons who
>
> - are suffering from grave chronic disease or being aged, infirm or physically incapacitated, are living in insanitary conditions, and
> - are unable to devote to themselves, and are not receiving from other persons, proper care and attention (National Assistance Act 1948, Section 47 (1)).

Fishwick (ibid.) then goes on to explain that:

> The power to apply for compulsory removal lies with the local authority on receiving medical confirmation from a person called the 'proper officer', who will normally be the community physician. If the proper officer certifies in writing to the appropriate authority that he is satisfied after thorough inquiry and consideration that in the interests of any such person or for preventing injury to the health of, or serious nuisance to, other persons, it is necessary to remove any such person the authority may apply to the magistrates' court (National Assistance Act 1948, Section 47 (2)).

Clearly, this describes a course of action which would only be used in extreme circumstances. However, it does illustrate a general feature of the policy context, namely that, in caring for people we may, at times, have to use measures of control. This is an important feature of the mental health legislation and it is to this that we now turn.

The Mental Health Act 1983

Once again we are dealing with a major piece of legislation with far-reaching implications. I shall therefore limit myself to discussion of three sections of the Act relating to compulsory admission to hospital and the section relating to guardianship. First, though, I shall 'set the scene' by commenting briefly on mental health policy in relation to older people.

An important issue in relation to mental health is the extent to which 'health' is to be interpreted metaphorically or literally (that is, as a medical matter). Indeed, the tension between the two conceptions of mental health is a recurring theme in the literature relating to mental disorder, and one we shall revisit in Chapters 4, 5 and 6. This tension is reflected in the Mental Health Act 1983 insofar as the Act attaches importance to both social and medical factors. For example, both social workers and doctors (GPs and psychiatrists) have a role to play in carrying out the statutory duties of the Act.

An important point to emerge from this is the danger of focusing exclusively or predominantly on medical matters, at the expense of social factors. This is particularly the case with regard to older people where the dehumanizing tendencies of ageism can lead to the neglect of broader social factors.

A second important policy theme is the tension between protecting the individual's rights and protecting others from harm. Again this is reflected within the Act, with a strong emphasis on rights in combination with the power to deprive individuals of their liberty in certain circumstances. Clearly, then, the combination of ageism and such significant powers can form the basis of a very oppressive form of practice in which rights are overlooked or only paid lip-service. The basic message, then, is that mental health matters must be addressed from an anti-ageist perspective if older people are not to be subjected to abuses of the law.

Compulsory admission to hospital is covered by various sections of the Act (hence the term 'sectioning') but the three main Sections are 2, 3 and 4. Section 2 relates to admission for assessment. McDonald and Taylor (1993) explain:

> The grounds are that the patient is suffering from mental disorder of a nature or degree which warrants his detention in a hospital for assessment (or for assessment followed by medical treatment) for a limited period of up to 28 days.

An application for admission must be founded on the written recommendations of two medical practitioners, one of whom must be approved as having special experience in the diagnosis and treatment of mental disorder and one of whom should, if practicable, have had previous acquaintance with the patient. The applicant must have personally seen the patient within the previous 14 days and admission must take place within 14 days of the date of the second medical examination. (p. 18)

The 'applicant' can be the nearest relative but is more likely to be an approved social worker (a social worker experienced in mental health work who has undertaken specialist training).

The procedure should apply only when the person's condition is such that he or she 'ought to be so detained in the interests of his own safety or with a view to the protection of others' (Ball, 1992, p. 88). It is, therefore, a provision which should be used only in exceptional circumstances, and should certainly not be seen as a means of forcing a reluctant service user to co-operate with a particular plan or course of action.

Section 3 parallels Section 2, except that the admission must be deemed necessary for treatment and can last for up to six months (at which point it may be renewed for a further six months). A Section 3 application often arises as the result of a Section 2 assessment but does not have to do so.

Practice focus 3.2

Mr Forrester had been admitted to hospital under Section 2 on three previous occasions due to 'psychotic episodes', periods of time when he seemed to lose all touch with reality. During these times he neglected his own safety and placed himself at considerable physical risk. On the fourth occasion, it was felt by the psychiatrist that no further assessment was needed, but an extended period of treatment would prove beneficial. She therefore recommended that the approved social worker apply for a Section 3 order.

Section 4 relates to emergency admissions and is to be used only where the delay in following the procedure for a Section 2 or 3 application could lead to harm to the person concerned or to other people. Unlike Sections 2 and 3, the application for compulsory admission in an emergency needs only one medical recommendation, rather than the usual two. A Section 4 admission lasts for a maximum of 72 hours, but can be 'converted' to a Section 2 if the second medical recommendation is obtained within the 72-hour period.

Section 4 is designed to be used strictly in emergencies only. The fact that it is inconvenient to obtain a second medical recommendation at short notice does not constitute an emergency situation. Once again, we need to be wary that the ageist tendency to see older people as a low priority does not lead to Section 4 applications being used as a short-cut.

Another important aspect of the Act is the possibility of an older person being made the subject of a Guardianship Order. This allows a Social Services Department or a named individual to act as a guardian. Brayne and Martin (1993) describe the procedure involved:

> Procedures for an application for guardianship are otherwise the same as admission for treatment . . . the nearest relative must be consulted and has the same power of veto; and there must be the two medical recommendations. (p. 263)

A Guardianship Order, which initially lasts for six months, is an alternative to hospital admission and gives the guardian certain powers to safeguard the individual and protect others:

> Under the 1983 Act, the guardian has the power to:
>
> (i)   require the patient to reside at a place specified;
> (ii) attend at places and times specified for the purpose of medical treatment, occupation, etc.;
> (iii) require that access to the patient may be given to any doctor, ASW or other similar person. (Ball, 1992, p. 92)

This is a provision not used very often, and when it is used it by no means guarantees success in achieving its aims. The situation therefore needs to be considered very carefully indeed before application is made for a Guardianship Order.

This is an Act which gives tremendous power to professionals, and therefore has the potential for making major changes to older people's lives, and these are not always changes for the better, despite the safeguards built into the Act. It is therefore important that staff working with older people have at least a basic awareness of the Act and its implications. The 'Code of Practice' for the Act provides a good account of expectations of good practice (Department of Health and Welsh Office, 1990).

Disability legislation

Where older people have a physical impairment, there are aspects of policy and legislation which apply. I shall give a brief overview of the main provisions.

The Chronically Sick and Disabled Persons Act 1970 imposes a duty on local authorities to assess the needs of disabled people within their area and to provide appropriate services. However, at a practical level, financial restrictions and a tendency for disabled people not to be seen as a priority (an example of disablism, parallel with ageism; see Oliver, 1983; Thompson, 1993) have led to a considerable shortfall in the provision of services and, in many areas, long waiting lists for an appointment with an occupational therapist or social worker. The Act also obliges local authorities to keep a register of disabled people. Being registered as disabled can be of benefit to disabled people in terms of access to welfare benefits and concessions.

According to McDonald and Taylor (1993), the Disabled Persons (Consultation and Representation) Act 1986:

> goes beyond the Chronically Sick and Disabled Persons Act 1970 in requiring local authorities to provide information not only about their own services but also about those services provided by other statutory and voluntary bodies concerned with disabled people. The Act also requires the needs of carers to be taken into account when the provision of services is being assessed. (p. 14)

It was also intended that local authorities would be obliged to appoint advocates to act on behalf of those disabled people who were unable to speak for themselves by virtue of their incapacity. However, this part of the Act has never been implemented, a further example of the marginalization of a minority group.

Other policy matters relating to disability have now been incorporated within the NHS and Community Care Act 1990 and so I shall return to these issues below when community care is discussed.

Protection of interests

There are a number of ways in which older people's interests can be safeguarded. I shall outline the main provisions here as an introduction to this important subject.

Protection of property

When a person is admitted to Part III accommodation, the local authority is obliged to safeguard personal property. This is usually achieved through a formal inventory of belongings. The provision even extends to making arrangements for pets where necessary. This obligation derives from the National Assistance Act 1948.

Court of Protection

Where it is not possible for a person to manage his or her own financial affairs by virtue of mental disorder, application can be made to the Court of Protection, an office of the Supreme Court, for a person to be appointed as a 'receiver' and manage the financial affairs. The receiver can be a friend, relative or representative of the local authority. This provision is, in some ways, similar to guardianship but relates specifically to managing finances.

Practice focus 3.3

Almost three years after being diagnosed as suffering from dementia, Mrs Sanderson was having great difficulty managing her finances due to her forgetfulness. Consequently, an application was made for a Court of Protection order. As a result of this order, Mrs Sanderson's niece was appointed as receiver. She then took day-to-day responsibility for her aunt's financial affairs and was entrusted to represent her interests without exploiting her in any way.

Power of attorney

If an older person wishes to appoint someone to act on his or her behalf in undertaking a financial transaction, this can be achieved through 'power of attorney', a written agreement which grants permission for the other person to manage the particular transaction.

Where the arrangement needs to apply on a longer-term basis, then 'enduring power of attorney' becomes applicable. As Fishwick (1992) comments:

> A power of attorney is a formal instrument by which one person authorises another to perform certain acts for him. An ordinary power of attorney loses its validity when the person creating it loses the mental capacity to manage his or her own affairs. An enduring power of attorney is a power of attorney which, subject to conditions and safeguards, continues in force even after the maker of the power (called 'the donor') becomes mentally incapable of handling his or her own affairs, provided that it is registered. (p. 166)

The donor must be mentally capable of understanding what the enduring power of attorney entails at the point at which it is made. When the person appointed as attorney believes that the donor is no longer mentally capable of managing his or her affairs, application needs to be made to the Court of Protection for the enduring power of attorney to be registered. Once registration is confirmed, the attorney is empowered to act on the donor's behalf for as long as is necessary.

Registration and inspection

Homes providing private residential care need to be registered with the local authority, and private nursing homes need to be registered with the local health authority. Such registration is a requirement of the Registered Homes Act 1984.

The aim of a registration is to ensure, as far as possible, that the facilities and standards of care offered are satisfactory. A home which fails to meet the required standards would not be allowed to operate. Standards in registered homes are kept under review by means of a programme of inspection visits. In this way, the State is playing a role in safeguarding the interests of older people who live in residential or nursing homes.

Community care

The National Health Service and Community Care Act 1990 came into force in April 1993 and has made a number of changes to the way care services are organized and delivered. Although this is a significant piece of legislation in terms of community care policy, it is a mistake to say that community care 'began' with the implementation of this Act. The concept of community care is a long-standing one and has influenced policy and provision over a period of decades. The Act is therefore the latest stage in a long process.

The Centre for Policy on Ageing (CPA, 1990) defines community care as 'that network of care which will maintain people, or where necessary, restore people to independent living. Customarily, this will be achieved by enabling them to live normally in their own homes' (p. 16). Community care, then, implies avoiding the need for institutional care wherever possible. There is, none the less, a strong argument that people in residential care could and should be more integrated into the local community. Independence is a matter of degree, rather than an 'all or nothing' concept.

The changes introduced by the Act include:

1 The local authority has primary responsibility for community care and is designated the 'lead authority'.
2 A great deal of funding which was previously allocated to different sources has now been centralized within the Social Services Department (SSD) budget.

3   Each local authority is obliged to produce a 'Community Care Plan', a
    document which is available to the general public. This document
    should cover services across the board and not simply those provided
    by the SSD.
4   The Act promotes the idea of a 'mixed economy of care'. There is to be
    less emphasis on the role of the SSD as a service provider by
    encouraging use of services available in the voluntary and private
    sectors.
5   Similarly, the Act distinguishes between service providers and service
    purchasers/commissioners. This introduces the role of the care
    manager, a person responsible for assessing need and co-ordinating
    service provision. The care manager is usually a local authority social
    worker but does not need to be.
6   The Act leads to less reliance on long-stay hospital care for older
    people, with a stronger focus on care within smaller community-based
    facilities such as nursing homes.
7   People who may be in need of community care services are entitled to
    an assessment of their needs. Upon request, the local authority is
    obliged to undertake an assessment in order to identify need and
    consider whether services are required and, if so, which ones. The
    assessment is therefore the basis of an individual 'care plan', a blueprint
    for what is necessary to maintain the person within the community.
8   Assessment should be 'needs-led'. That is, the assessment should be
    more than a simple rationing of available services (service-led assess-
    ment). Needs should be identified, regardless of whether suitable
    services are available to meet them. A needs-led assessment is
    necessary in order to:

    –   identify shortfall of services;
    –   provide a basis for planning service developments;
    –   stimulate an imaginative and creative use of existing resources.

    Needs-led assessment is not a new concept, but it is now seen as a basic
    expectation of good practice.

These are by no means the only changes to be introduced but it is beyond
the scope of this book to provide a comprehensive overview.

    Seed and Kaye (1994) distinguish between the policy of community care
which is premised on factors such as closing down long-stay hospitals and
a quest for value for money, and the philosophy of community care which
is premised on:

1   *'Quality of life'*. Quality of life criteria should be adopted for assessing
    people's needs for support in personal care and daily living in the

---

Practice focus 3.4

Martin began his placement with the Adult Services Team with only a vague understanding of the legal requirements of the NHS and Community Care Act 1990. However, as he was keen to do a good job, he read a great deal about the subject and followed the procedures closely. This proved to be very helpful as he was able to undertake needs-led assessments systematically without being influenced by traditional service-led practices.

---

community. 'Quality of life' includes material, social and spiritual well being in a safe environment.

2 *Individualisation*. An integrated and individualised response to assessed needs on the part of health and social services.

3 *Participation*. A participatory approach to the provision of services, emphasising personal choice.

4 *Developing potential*. Building on existing or potential sources of support from relatives, friends, neighbourhood resources and other components of people's social networks. (Seed and Kaye, 1994, p. 5)

This is an important distinction as it illustrates how professional concerns (the four elements of good practice in the quotation above, for example) and political interest (reducing costs and altering the role of the State, for example) combine within a particular policy. The danger, then, is that the political interests are allowed to predominate at the expense of professional values and concerns. Indeed, this is an important point in relation to the policy context more generally – the need to ensure that professional practice does not become simply a 'political pawn'. Political power is not to be underestimated, but this is not to say that staff, both individually and collectively, do not have a part to play in influencing policy through its interpretation and implementation.

Community care, then, is a complex and major part of the policy context and one which merits close attention. However, this brief introductory overview must be limited to a consideration of some of the dangers inherent in current approaches to community care, three in particular:

1 *Underfunding*: A common fallacy about community care is that it is a cheap option, a means of reducing care costs. Furthermore, the focus on needs-led assessment also has the effect of revealing layers of need which traditional assessment practices left unrevealed. The consequence of this can be a raising of expectations combined with a relative tightening of the purse strings, thereby producing considerable dissatisfaction.

2   *Sexism*: Finch and Groves (1983) discuss the 'double equation' of community care – care by the community equals care by the family, and care by the family equals care by women. That is, we need to recognize that community care places tremendous pressure on carers and, as the majority of carers are women, this raises significant issues with regard to sexism. This is a point to which we shall return in Chapter 7.

3   *A service ethos*: One criticism of work with older people is that it can easily become a routine matching of need to services available (Thompson, 1989). The new emphasis on needs-led assessment has helped to counter this tendency. However, what can still remain is a 'service ethos', an almost exclusive focus on providing services. Other aspects of intervention such as 'use of self' can be pushed into the background by an overemphasis on service delivery. This raises important issues which will be discussed in more detail in Chapter 5.

Clearly, then, community care represents a very complex set of issues and will remain a subject of debate and dispute for many years to come as we wrestle with some very thorny matters of policy, politics and practice.

Conclusion

The policy context of work with older people has many dimensions and many levels. It is a subject matter which would repay detailed and extensive study. However, it would be unrealistic to attempt to go beyond the basics within this text. It is to be hoped that the discussions here will act as both a stimulus and a gateway to further study and better understanding, thereby leading, potentially at least, to higher standards of practice.

In sum, the key points to be emphasized in drawing this chapter to a close are:

- Practice does not occur in a vacuum – it happens in the context of policy, law, history and politics.
- Good practice requires us to be aware of legal powers, duties and expectations.
- The policy context poses a number of problems, dilemmas and challenges. There is a need for us to engage critically with law and policy and not simply take it at face value.

These, and other issues, are important factors in influencing work with older people and will therefore re-emerge at various points in the chapters that follow.

4 Dealing with difficulties

Introduction

This is the first of two chapters to address the problems encountered by older people and the steps that can be taken to solve, reduce or alleviate them. This chapter concentrates primarily on the problems experienced, albeit with some discussion of actions that can be taken. Chapter 5 complements this by shifting the emphasis to the 'professional task', the actual tasks and duties facing staff who work with older people. Once again, the focus is on working within an anti-ageist framework, in terms of both understanding the nature of the problems or difficulties and making an appropriate response to them.

The chapter basically consists of a discussion of a range of difficulties staff commonly come across in working with older people. An important point to emphasize, though, is that, in focusing on problems and difficulties, we should not fall into the trap of seeing old age as a problem in itself. For example, we must be careful to avoid making statements such as the following:

> Greater life expectancy, which has occurred mainly through a fall in infant mortality, raises considerable problems. The average cost of health and welfare services for an old person is about seven times that of a person of working age. (Byrne and Padfield, 1985, p. 94)

The ageist notion that older people are an unfortunate burden is clearly implied by seeing greater life expectancy as a source of problems, rather than a positive benefit.

An important part of dealing with problems is to be clear who they are problems for. This helps to avoid confusing the problems of older people

61

with the ageist notion of older people as a problem. This also helps to avoid the classic error of assessment (to be discussed in Chapter 5) where possible actions are discussed, or even implemented, without first clarifying the nature or extent of the problem.

The overview of problems presented in this chapter is therefore intended as an aid to assessment, a means of helping staff to understand at least the basics of some of the difficulties that many older people experience. However, it should be stressed that an aid to assessment is no substitute for assessment – understanding the basics of a problem is only the beginning of a process, not the end.

I shall outline, in turn, a number of common problems before presenting a concluding discussion that draws together some of the unifying themes.

Internalized oppression

In Chapter 2 the point was made that ageism exists not only at a social level, but becomes internalized at an individual level. That is, the negative images projected by the ideology of ageism become part of the individual's self-image and this, in turn, influences thoughts, feelings, actions and interactions. This reflects the broader process by which a range of social factors become internalized as part of the individual's sense of self and his or her perspective on the world.

The negative beliefs and values upon which ageism is founded form an ideology which influences not only those who have yet to reach old age but also older people themselves. This is captured in the comments of Scrutton (1989) when he argues that:

> Ageism associates old age very closely with pain. It is tacitly accepted that elderly people become increasingly prone to sickness and ill-health. To an extent this is based on truth. However, ageism takes what is a normal tendency and transforms it into an extreme and depressing inevitability. Thus, arthritis will progressively wrack their bodies with pain. Their heart and other vital organs will decline in vigour and vitality in an inevitable process of wasting, leading to a series of ailments for which there is little defence. As bodily functions decrease, constipation, incontinence and other conditions will increase. They will lose control of their limbs, muscles will weaken and their sense of balance will diminish. Sight and hearing will fail. The process is pre-ordained, and little can be done to halt the inevitability of personal decline and ill-health. (p. 20)

This ideology presents old age as if it were some form of illness in itself, thus reflecting a common characteristic of oppressive ideologies – a tendency to draw on pseudo-biological justifications for presenting certain social groups in an unduly negative light. But another significant aspect of ideology is its ability to 'interpellate' – that is, its ability to win people over and become an integral part of their thoughts and attitudes. Thus, there is a danger that older people may accept too readily the overly negative conception of old age inherent in ageist ideology.

The dominance of ageist stereotypes can therefore lead older people to subscribe to the myth that old age is primarily a period of illness and incapability. Where this occurs it can lead to a number of problems:

- a lack of confidence;
- low self-esteem (see the discussion of depression later in this chapter);
- a reluctance to seek medical assistance when required (pain and suffering are seen as 'par for the course');
- a tendency to see oneself as a nuisance or a burden if some form of assistance or care is required;
- guilt about taking up other people's time or attention;
- difficulties in maintaining a positive thread of meaning in one's life.

Practice focus 4.1

Mrs Pearson had worked as the headteacher of a primary school before retirement some 22 years ago. She had been confident, assertive and proud of her achievements. However, when she was admitted to hospital with a chest infection, the nursing staff encountered a very different person. She came across as a very shy person, almost totally lacking in confidence. She apologized constantly for 'being a nuisance'. Her experiences of old age had taken away much of the spirit that had helped make her earlier life such a success.

Of course, not all older people experience all of these problems, but the significant role of internalized oppression is one practitioners should not neglect – we can so easily reinforce negative feelings if we are not sensitive to them, if we do not appreciate how the structures of ageism apply not only 'out there' in the social world, but also 'in here' in the subjective life-world of the individual. There is, therefore, a need for staff working with older people to understand the nature of internalized ageist oppression and be prepared to counter its insidious and destructive effects.

Depression

Some of the factors commonly associated with depression are:

- loss and bereavement;
- frustrated aggression;
- low self-esteem;
- helplessness;
- difficulty in sustaining meaning, purpose and value.

These are factors which are, to some extent at least, also associated with old age. It is perhaps not surprising, then, that there is a strong association between old age and depression.

In Chapter 2, the point was made that old age is a time characterized by loss for a variety of reasons. Old age is also expected to be a time of serenity and acceptance, and so expressions of anger and aggression do not receive social approval. Such feelings may therefore have to be 'swallowed' and absorbed.

We have also seen how internalized oppression contributes to a negative self-image and low self-esteem. This combination of factors, together with the overall demeaning effects of ageism, can be instrumental in making it difficult for older people to sustain a thread of meaning, purpose and value.

Practice focus 4.2

Ella was a bereavement counsellor with a voluntary organization. When Mrs Stanford, aged 79, was referred to her following her husband's death, she approached the task with enthusiasm as she had had a lot of success with older people in the past. It did not take Ella long to recognize a particular aspect of Mrs Stanford's experience – the profound sense of loss of role. Since her retirement, and indeed before that to a large extent, her husband had been a central figure in her life. Her social life had revolved around him and she had few interests of her own. Now that he was no longer with her, Mrs Stanford was going to need a lot of help in developing a new sense of direction, a new world of meaning without her husband.

Windmill (1990) comments on common causes of depression in old age, although, significantly, she does not include ageism as a factor:

Depression is a condition that can affect any age group, but the elderly [*sic*] are prone to depression as old age is often accompanied by loneliness, ill-health, bereavement, lack of money and loss of status in society: all situations which are potentially likely to cause depression in anyone. Depression may also be caused by any of these situations.

- Physical causes such as:

    (i)   having recently had an operation
    (ii)   illness, especially viral infections
    (iii)   head injuries
    (iv)   brain disorders such as stroke or epilepsy
    (v)   hormonal fluctuations during and after the menopause

- Social causes such as:

    (i)   loneliness and isolation, e.g., the elderly living alone
    (ii)   lack of money resulting in loss of status
    (iii)   bereavement
    (iv)   family changes, e.g., close family moving away (p. 22)

One important point to note with regard to depression in old age is the danger of seeing 'symptoms' that are not there. For example, insomnia and loss of appetite are commonly associated with depression, but a tendency to sleep and eat less in the later years is not at all unusual or problematic. We therefore need to be careful not to assume that an older person is depressed simply on these grounds. As we shall see in the next chapter, a more thorough assessment is called for.

A distinction is commonly made between 'reactive' depression, where the cause is relatively clear (a reaction to bereavement, for example) and 'endogenous' depression, where there is no apparent direct cause. This can arguably be seen as a tenuous distinction in general, but in relation to older people specifically, it becomes even more problematic. Old age is characteristically seen, from an ontological point of view, as a time of life review and so it is difficult to know what factors have been significant in leading to depression – the life review process may have triggered off memories of one or more painful experiences, or brought home how much has been lost from one's earlier life.

A final point to note with regard to depression in old age is that, whilst depression overall is not significantly more prevalent in older people than amongst any other age group (Murphy, 1993), it is quite closely associated with residential care:

Old people living in old people's homes or nursing homes are more likely to suffer from depression than people living in their own homes. As many as one-third of the residents of such homes in Britain are suffering in this way. We do not know if the environment and quality of life in these institutions are the cause of the problem. (p. 95)

Whilst the problem of depression in old age is one that all staff need to understand and be sensitive to, the challenge for staff working in residential care is clearly a significant one.

Communication difficulties

Communication difficulties can arise for a wide variety of reasons, including the following:

- hearing impairment;
- stroke or other physical infirmity;
- dementia;
- depression;
- fear, anxiety or mistrust;
- linguistic differences.

With regard to hearing impairments, it is necessary to recognize that:

1   A degree of hearing loss does not automatically lead to problems of communication.
2   Where it is necessary to raise one's voice in speaking to a person with a hearing impairment, this should be achieved by raising volume without altering pitch. That is, speaking more loudly is not the same as shouting. The former can be helpful; the latter is demeaning.
3   Care must be taken not to fall into the ageist trap of assuming that all or most older people have a hearing impairment.

In the case of a stroke or other physical infirmity, difficulties are more likely to relate to producing speech, rather than hearing it. Such situations can be complex and demanding but, in particular, two points should be noted:

1   We should beware of an over-reliance on speech. A more creative and imaginative approach to communication may be called for, perhaps using writing, non-verbal communication or computer technology.
2   Difficulty in issuing a communication should not be equated with being unable to receive communications. That is, the fact that someone cannot respond to what is said does not mean that it has not been heard. Indeed, this applies to other forms of communication difficulty too.

Dementia presents a range of problems, including communication difficulties, and these require special attention. Chapter 6 is devoted to issues related to dementia, including the question of communication.

Depression, with its flattening of mood and affect, can also inhibit communication. In such cases, great skill and patience may be required in order to communicate effectively – with the right tone, at the right pace and so on.

Fear, anxiety or mistrust are, understandably, barriers to communication insofar as they create tensions that stand in the way of the sort of relationship that promotes good communication. For staff working with older people, fear, anxiety and mistrust are often the starting point as these feelings are characteristically engendered by ageism. That is, the negative effects of ageism can lead older people to feel mistrustful, fearful or anxious, particularly in relation to people who may appear to have some degree of power over them, nurses or social workers, for example. Anti-ageist practice therefore needs to take account of these potential barriers for, unless we acknowledge the significance of ageism in this respect, we may fall into the trap of misreading the feelings encountered and attributing them to other causes. For example, we may see a person as being unduly anxious without appreciating the role of ageism in leading him or her to feel anxious in our presence.

Linguistic differences may be so great as to require the assistance of an interpreter. For example, where a person has little or no grasp of the English language, there may be little point in attempting to communicate without the intermediary of an interpreter. However, even where an older person is very fluent in English, if English is not his or her first language the potential for communication difficulties may exist (Pugh, 1994). For example, a person whose first language is Welsh may be very fluent in English but may not feel entirely comfortable discussing certain things (personal care, perhaps) in his or her second language and this, in turn, may inhibit positive communication.

Without doubt, then, communication problems can be major obstacles to a positive and dignified experience of old age. The need to be sensitive to issues of communication is therefore a central feature of good practice in working with older people.

Elder abuse

The abuse of older people is a topic that has received far more attention in North America than it has in Britain. Indeed, the extent and significance of the problem has yet to be fully appreciated by care professionals, let alone the general public.

There has been much debate about a precise definition of elder abuse (or 'old age abuse' as it is also called) but the recognition that it is a problem to be taken seriously by all staff working with older people is far less open to dispute. It is therefore important that staff have at least a basic understanding of elder abuse.

The abuse of older people can take five basic forms (McCreadie, 1994). These are:

1 *Physical abuse*: This refers to physical harm inflicted on an older person and resulting in pain, injury or injuries.
2 *Psychological abuse*: This term covers verbal abuse, threat, humiliation or other forms of emotional cruelty.
3 *Sexual abuse*: This includes any form of inappropriate sexual contact or activity brought about through pressure or coercion.
4 *Financial abuse*: This involves the financial exploitation of an older person by a person in a position of trust.
5 *Neglect*: This applies to situations in which a person who is reliant on someone else for care does not receive adequate care to meet basic needs.

There can be some degree of overlap between these forms of abuse. For example, the psychological abuse of bullying can easily spill over into physical abuse or come very close to it (perhaps by pushing, holding or shaking). Also, different forms of abuse can occur at the same time for the same person. In fact, it is possible for someone to experience all five forms of abuse within the same situation. That is, they are not mutually exclusive.

In this respect, elder abuse has much in common with child abuse. However, what differs significantly from child abuse is the absence, in the UK at least, of a statutory duty to investigate, and respond to, instances or allegations of abuse against an elderly person. In law, policy and practice, a vulnerable older person has far less protection than a vulnerable child, a considerable irony in view of the tendency towards infantilization identified in Chapter 1.

What older people do share with children, however, are the effects of marginalization brought about by ageism. Indeed, ageism can be seen to be a significant factor in elder abuse, as Biggs and Phillipson (1994) recognize when they argue that: 'An important principle to convey to workers is that the mistreatment of older people starts from the initial experience of ageism within society' (p. 215). Jack (1994) pursues a similar line of argument when he emphasizes the sense of powerlessness experienced by older people within a society characterized by ageism. In discussing the role of ageist stereotypes in the context of elder abuse, he quotes Solomon (1983):

> By stereotyping the aged person as dependent, senile, incompetent and chronically disordered with a poor prognosis, the health worker does not respond to the older person's behaviour and needs but responds to the patient's custodial or maintenance needs, as perceived by the worker. These perceptions are frequently different from the patient's own perception of his needs . . . the older patient's individuality and individual needs become lost to the provider. (cited in Jack, 1994, p. 83)

Jack points out that this process leads to helplessness and powerlessness, but it can also be seen to lead to dehumanization, the dehumanization inherent in ageism that leads to older people being treated as less than full citizens.

In view of this, developing anti-ageist practice can be seen as a basic component in the prevention of elder abuse, a means of guarding against the 'slippery slope' of which Stevenson (1989) writes:

> There is a terrifying slippery slope in the process, by which old people come to be regarded as less than fully human and are not therefore treated as persons deserving equal respect. This may be exacerbated by their mental frailty or by their neglected appearance (a vicious circle in this context) or by sensory deficits such as deafness. (p. 23)

Whilst appreciating the significance of ageism gives us the beginnings of an understanding of the causal factors underpinning elder abuse, we must recognize that we are only in the early stages of developing a theory of elder abuse that explains:

- the factors that lead to abuse;
- the factors that inhibit or prevent abuse;
- the social and psychological factors that affect the perpetrator;
- the relationship between the different forms of abuse;
- the longer-term effects of abuse on both the victim and the perpetrator;

and so on.

It is important that we acknowledge that we are in the very early stages of theory development for, as McCreadie (1994) comments: 'One general implication of the research is that elder abuse is a complex subject and one where we should be wary of stereotypes and simplistic explanations' (p. 4).

One such simplistic explanation is the view that abuse is necessarily associated with high levels of dependency. Bennett and Kingston (1993) question this assumption when they comment that:

Elders that were abused were not considered more functionally disabled or ill than the control group, and surprisingly in certain areas were less impaired. The abused group were not more dependent on their carer than the non-abused group in activities of daily living (ADL). (p. 19)

Similarly, there is a danger that the limited knowledge we have gained may be overextended to the point where it becomes distorted, and thereby hides more than it reveals. For example, as Hocking (1994) illustrates, pressure on over-burdened carers can lead to abuse: 'Abusing carers have lost control of the situation themselves and their emotions. Amid the chaos, they feel frustrated, embarrassed, angry and powerless' (p. 51). However, it would be a mistake to see the overstressed carer scenario as the only one, thereby failing to take account of other explanations or abusive situations, such as:

- mental health problems in the carer;
- responses to family discord, currently or in the past;
- a history of violence on the part of the carer;
- opportunities for financial gain, perhaps combined with debt on the carer's part;
- alcohol or other substance abuse.

This is not to deny the significance of pressure on carers (as I shall emphasize in Chapter 7) but should sensitize us to the range of other circumstances that have a part to play.

Practice focus 4.3

Eluned had become aware of elder abuse through running a support group for carers and appreciating the dangers of excessive strain. However, it was only when she attended a training course on elder abuse that she came to appreciate the wide range of factors that could contribute to abusive situations. She heard colleagues give examples of unresolved family feuds; drunken outbursts; violence related to mental health problems; deliberate, calculated theft of money and valuables; and a number of other varied circumstances that resulted in abuse. From this, Eluned learned that elder abuse is a complex subject that needs careful and sensitive handling.

Finally, in relation to elder abuse, the point needs to be emphasized that abuse does not take place only in families or in the community. It would be naive not to recognize that abuse also occurs in institutional settings

(Gilleard, 1994). It is therefore essential that we are not complacent about abuse, and are prepared to be vigilant about the potential for abuse even within a caring environment.

Disability and disabling illnesses

Whilst the incidence of disability and disabling illnesses is higher in the older population than it is amongst younger people (Victor, 1991), this fact should not be misinterpreted as confirmation that old age is a form of disability in its own right. As Qureshi and Walker (1986) point out, the incidence of illness and infirmity in old age is grossly exaggerated. The tendency to associate impairment with old age is a further reflection of the negative tendencies of ageism.

However, we do need to recognize that many older people are prone to disability or disabling illnesses such as rheumatism or arthritis. This means that a balance is called for. We need to avoid the two extremes, one which equates old age with disability, and the other which underestimates the significant problems many older people encounter.

This constructive balance involves recognizing, and implementing, the steps necessary for minimizing the negative effects of an impairment or a disabling illness. These steps can be seen to fall into three categories:

1 *Environmental*: Changes to the individual's environment such as aids, adaptations and related services can have a significant role to play.
2 *Sociopolitical*: This involves countering disablism, a form of oppression parallel with ageism (see below).
3 *Psychological*: Just as ageism manifests itself in the form of internalized oppression and low self-esteem, so too can disablism. Work may therefore need to be done to empower older people to overcome the negative mind-set associated with disablism.

Disablism can be defined as:

the combination of social forces, cultural values and personal prejudices which marginalises disabled people, portrays them in a negative light and thus oppresses them. This combination encapsulates a powerful ideology which has the effect of denying disabled people full participation in mainstream social life . . . Disablism shares many of the features of ageism: a tendency towards infantilisation, a patronising 'does she take sugar?' attitude, an assumption of illness and so on. (Thompson, 1993, p. 105)

For older people who become disabled and for disabled people as they grow older (Zarb, 1993), both ageism and disablism can be experienced.

The interaction of the two forms of oppression can produce a dynamic which engenders a range of problems for the people so affected. That is, discrimination on the grounds of age combines with discrimination against disabled people to produce a potentially doubly disadvantaged situation for disabled older people.

Oliver (1990) makes the point that disability is a social disadvantage; that is, the physical impairment that gives rise to the disability is exacerbated and amplified by the social response to the impairment. This is parallel with ageism, as discussed in Chapter 2, in that problems at a biological level are amplified by social attitudes, values and institutional practices. Disablism therefore produces what Davis (1986) calls 'disabled apartheid', a situation in which disabled people are marginalized, dehumanized and disempowered.

One important consequence of this for practitioners is the need to avoid reinforcing disablist stereotypes (see Oliver, 1983; Thompson, 1993, Ch. 6) as these can add an extra burden of oppression to the ageism older people already encounter.

Incontinence

The first point to note is that incontinence is not an inevitable consequence of ageing. Consequently, where and when it does occur, it should be seen as a problem to be investigated and dealt with, rather than a destiny that has to be accepted and tolerated.

Wellings (1991) provides a useful framework in which continence (of urine) can be seen to entail being able to:

- identify a suitable place to pass urine
- reach that place
- retain urine until voiding is desired. (p.74)

Incontinence can result when any one of these three is not achieved. For example, a disorder such as dementia may lead to problems in identifying a suitable place. Similarly, mobility problems may prevent a person reaching the appropriate place in time. In addition, being able to retain urine until voiding is desired may be prevented by infection or other physical causes. In trying to deal with problems of incontinence, then, this threefold framework can be very helpful in identifying the area in which the problem lies and thereby provide a focus for trying to rectify the problem.

Wellings's model relates specifically to incontinence of urine but the same framework can also be seen to apply to incontinence of faeces.

Incontinence can arise from a wide range of causes, including infection, prolapsed uterus, enlarged prostate, loss of central nervous system control, Parkinsonism, constipation, ulcerative colitis and the side-effects of drug treatments. An important point to recognize, in view of the wide range of potential causes, is that incontinence needs to be thoroughly investigated, rather than taken for granted as an inherent part of the ageing process. Such an investigation is of central importance as it allows medical staff to identify possible ways of rectifying the problem (antibiotics for an infection, exercise to strengthen muscles, or surgery) or managing it (habit reinforcement, regular reminders, inco-pads and so on) in order to minimize the pain and distress involved (Bennett and Ebrahim, 1992).

However, while the medical dimension is clearly an important one, once again we need to be wary of allowing medical or biological aspects to dominate or overshadow significant psychological or social features of the situation. That is, in addition to the medical factors, an assessment needs to cover:

- *Emotional factors that may be having an influence on the situation*: Grief, conflict, anxiety and stress can all play a significant part and therefore need to be taken into consideration.
- *Attitudes of, and towards, the person concerned*: Feelings of shame, disgust or even anger can have a bearing on the situation and how it is dealt with.
- *The degree and nature of support*: To what extent a person will be able to maintain continence will depend, in part at least, on the support networks to which he or she has access.
- *Environmental barriers*: Continence can be helped or hindered by the physical environment in which the older person exists. In many cases, adjustments to the environment can make a significant difference in a person's ability to remain continent.

Whilst this is not an exhaustive list, it does give an indication of the range of factors above and beyond the medical dimension. Underpinning all these factors, though, is one central factor – the importance of helping an older person maintain a sense of dignity and self-respect. Incontinence is a serious challenge to this, and so it is essential that the response of staff in such situations is one that promotes dignity, rather than undermines it.

Aggression

The question of aggression and violence towards older people has already been discussed under the heading of 'Elder abuse'. However, what also needs to be considered is the question of aggression on the part of older people.

Harvey (1990) defines aggression in the following terms:

> This may take the form of verbal abuse or physical violence towards another person. Such behaviour is often particularly difficult for others. If the behaviour is seen as a personal threat, fear within can cloud the ability to assert the skills that are necessary to deal with the situation. (p. 20)

Aggression can be a problem for:

- direct carers who may bear the brunt of negative feelings and hostile actions;
- indirect carers such as community nurses, health visitors, social workers and so on who may be called upon to find a solution to the problem;
- the person concerned, as a result of tension, conflict, guilt, breakdown of relationships and so on;
- the spouse, friends or others who are not direct carers but none the less have an interest in the older person's welfare.

The causes of aggression are many and varied, including the following:

- *Frustration, tension, conflict and anger*: That is, the situations that lead to aggression for younger adults can also do so for older people. Indeed, some of the situations that lead to frustration may be more prevalent in old age.
- *Disorders such as dementia*: Note, however, that aggression is by no means an inevitable consequence of dementia.
- *Ageism*: A response to its inherent indignities, marginalization and infantilization.
- *A strategy for coping*: If people have tended to resort to violence in response to pressure and stress in their earlier lives, then this pattern may well continue into old age.
- *The effects of drugs*: This may be as a result of the disinhibiting effects of alcohol or, less frequently, the adverse side-effects of drug treatments.

Incidents of aggression can be very upsetting for all concerned and so strategies for preventing such incidents are well worth developing. In this regard, there are important points to note:

- The potential for aggressive outbursts is often signalled through behaviours or non-verbal signs that differ from the norm. That is, a sensitivity to the 'signals' that can precede aggression is worth developing.

Practice focus 4.4

It was an extraordinary coincidence that Sheila and Terri, two members of staff at the same residential home, were both attacked on the same day. However, the circumstances leading to the two incidents were very different indeed. Sheila was struck by Mr Jones, a man whose earlier life had been characterized by violence, a fact reflected in his criminal record and the breakdown of his marriage. Terri, by contrast, was kicked by Mrs Tate, a normally placid person who had shown no previous signs of aggression, but who was becoming increasingly frustrated and agitated. Ironically, both Sheila and Terri felt guilty about what part they may have played in provoking the attacks.

- Aggression is situational. Aggression is not a 'flaw' in an individual, it is a response to a situation. Understanding the situational factors associated with aggression is therefore an important part of preventing problematic situations arising. There may be significant 'triggers' that can be identified.
- We need to be sensitive to our own responses as well as the older person's. As More (1990) comments: 'Understanding what is happening to the aggressor is only part of what is necessary; we must also appreciate what is happening to us when we are faced with the angry or violent client or the attacking stranger' (p. 19).

One final point to stress with regard to aggression is the danger of focusing on actual or potential incidents of violence at the expense of dealing effectively with the aftermath of such experiences. The 'aftermath' needs to be considered at two levels:

1 For the worker involved – traumatic incidents can be very stressful, particularly if not handled sensitively afterwards (Thompson *et al.*, 1994).
2 For service users (including carers) – the upsetting effects of aggression can be intense and long-lasting, and counselling or other forms of help may be needed.

Conclusion

It will be evident from this chapter that older people face a significant range of problems and difficulties. However, we need to be wary of adopting too negative a perspective on old age. It is important that we keep things in proportion and recognize that the issues addressed here are potential problems and by no means apply to all, or even most, older people.

None the less, where people do experience one or more of the problems outlined here, the negative and destructive effects on quality of life can be of major proportions. The need for human services workers to take them very seriously should therefore be firmly established.

The problems described here are by no means the only ones. Indeed, at least one major problem – poverty – has not been discussed at all, and yet its effects can be extreme. But, even in its less extreme forms, poverty can exacerbate and complicate other problems. For example, poverty can lead to tensions that trigger aggression or feelings of helplessness that underpin depression. Poverty can therefore be seen as not only a problem in its own right, but also a significant dimension of a range of other problems.

Poverty is a reflection of socioeconomic class and is therefore part of the social structure. As such, it takes its place alongside such important issues as racism, sexism and, of course, ageism. The significance of poverty as a factor in many older people's lives reinforces the important point made in Chapter 1 that we need to look beyond the individual to take into account broader cultural and structural factors. If we do not expand our perspective beyond the individual to take into account broader cultural and structural factors, then we run the risk of failing to recognize some very significant influences on the individual's thoughts, feelings and actions, and the problems he or she encounters. Ironically, then, we cannot understand the individual simply by focusing on the individual – the context has to be taken into account.

Having reviewed, then, some of the main problems and difficulties that older people can experience, attention now needs to focus on what can be done by health and social welfare professionals to promote a positive quality of life and make a contribution to countering ageism and its insidious damage. This is precisely the task of Chapter 5 – to map out the main features of the professional task and highlight some of the key issues that contribute to, or stand in the way of, good practice.

5 The professional task

Introduction

The aim of this chapter is to consider what needs to be done in working with older people and explore what constitutes good practice. To a certain extent, then, this entails identifying examples of bad practice and, in so doing, highlighting the pitfalls that practitioners are to be wary of if high-quality practice is to be achieved.

This is not to say that this chapter will provide the 'right answers'. It would be naive to assume that the 'right answers' can be achieved outside the context of actual practice. It is also misleading to assume that 'right answers' exist if, by this, we mean foolproof formulae that guarantee success. Good practice relies upon theory, but understanding theory does not, in itself, bring success. Applying theory to practice is a skilled activity (Thompson, 1995b), and so the best that can be achieved in a chapter such as this is a basis for good practice.

Five broad areas are discussed here. First, care management is explained and some common misunderstandings are clarified. This is followed by an overview of assessment, outlining what it involves and, in particular, emphasizing the need for it to be done thoroughly and effectively. Next comes a consideration of counselling and its role in problem-solving and promoting quality of life. This leads into a discussion of advocacy and mediation and the importance of safeguarding rights. Finally, the question of creative methods is addressed and the value of an imaginative approach is elaborated upon.

But, before tackling these five sets of issues, some prefatory remarks are called for. First, we need to challenge and reject the notion that working with older people is simply a matter of common sense, and only requires caring people with their hearts in the right place. This notion is not only

77

wrong (it underestimates the demands, complexities and challenges involved in working with older people), it is also dangerous, insofar as it tends to reinforce the ageist tendency to devalue older people and see their needs as simple and straightforward.

Second, it has to be acknowledged that not all staff will be engaged in each of the five areas of practice outlined here. However, I would argue that, in order to provide the best possible level of service, it is necessary for each group of staff to understand at least the basics of what tasks other staff groups undertake in playing their part in working with older people. Effective multidisciplinary work is premised on each set of workers appreciating the roles, tasks and pressures of the other staff involved so that misunderstandings and tensions are kept to a minimum.

Third, the tasks discussed here are not the only ones that play an important part in good practice. Space does not permit a comprehensive account, and so, inevitably, a number of important aspects have had to be omitted. The fact that a particular issue is not discussed here should therefore not be seen to imply that it is not important.

Care management

Care management is a concept and form of practice that has come to prominence in recent years due, in no small part, to the implementation of the National Health Service and Community Care Act 1990 (NHSCCA). It is closely linked to the American concept of *case* management. Indeed, in the debates and planning that led up to the NHSCCA, the two terms were often used interchangeably.

Care management is an approach to practice closely associated with community care. It is based on the view that, through an appropriate assessment of needs and the effective and efficient use of available resources to meet those needs, the need for institutional care could be avoided or kept to a minimum. The care manager is therefore a central figure in community care.

The care manager has a significant role to play in co-ordinating services and ensuring, as far as possible, that the resources available are used to optimal effect. The Centre for Policy on Ageing (CPA) guide *Community Life* also comments on the co-ordinating role as part of 'consumer liaison':

> Where there is only one worker involved this will be straightforward. However, where there are several services being provided it is good practice that one person be placed in a co-ordinating role and that the user should know to whom to turn if things go wrong or if there is a need to review the arrangements. (1990, p. 33)

A co-ordinating role is also important with regard to the 'mixed economy of welfare' that is encouraged by current community care arrangements. That is, the increasing role of the voluntary and private sectors makes for a more diverse range of services, and thus increases the need for a co-ordinator to oversee service provision in order to prevent a chaotic jumble of services and/or significant gaps – to ensure a coherent care plan.

In addition to co-ordination, the care manager's role can be seen to include:

- Assessment – this is discussed in more detail in the next section.
- Establishing priorities – available resources are, of course, limited, and so decisions have to be made about priority levels so that the more important needs are met first.
- Planning a care package – Orme and Glastonbury (1993) define a care package in the following terms:

> Once a person's assessment is completed there is a process of identifying whether that person's needs warrant service provision (matters like statutory responsibility and the availability of resources come in here) and if a high enough priority is agreed then appropriate services are sought. Within care management, services should be carefully planned, identified and established to meet the assessed needs of the client. Services set up in this way form the care package. (p. 187)

- Contributing to resource allocation – some care managers have direct budgetary control whilst others have to make application elsewhere for funds, for example to a service manager.
- Overseeing service provision and reviewing needs – changes of circumstance may require modifications to the care package. It is therefore important that monitoring and review take place.

Practice focus 5.1

After a visit from her GP, Mrs Russell was referred to a care manager. When Pauline, the care manager, made her first visit, she 'set out her stall' by explaining her role and what it entailed. She described to Mrs Russell how she would work with her to identify what she needed and then try to put together a 'care package', a set of measures intended to meet those needs as far as possible within the resources available. The clear and simple explanation provided by the care manager reassured Mrs Russell, removed much of the mystique about what would happen, and gave her a great deal of confidence in Pauline.

These, then, are among the basic tasks of the care manager. Like many roles in the caring professions, it can easily be oversimplified and reduced to its lowest common denominator, or even distorted beyond recognition. There is a danger that the care manager becomes an uncritical form-filler and a routine rationer of resources, particularly if training and supervision are not available while demand continues to rise in a context of diminishing resources.

This raises the question, then, of what care management should be like in ideal circumstances. A full answer to such a question would require a major work in its own right. However, the following points are likely to feature in such an answer:

- Skilled, sensitive and well-informed assessment practices are needed, rather than routine information gathering.
- A creative and imaginative approach is called for so that the potential of older people and their carers can be enhanced and developed. This avoids getting stuck in the rut of a simplistic service provision. For example, an alteration to the older person's environment may avoid the need to provide services at all, or reduce the level of service needed.
- A participative approach based on user-involvement is to be preferred to one in which service users are expected to play a passive role. That is, practice needs to be based on partnership, rather than paternalism (Thompson, 1992a), so that dependency is not created.
- Whilst it is recognized that practice has to be finance-limited due to inevitable constraints of specific budgets and overall levels of health and welfare spending, this is not to say that it should be finance-led. That is, within a limited budget, cost has to be an important factor. However, it should not be allowed to become the primary one.
- Similarly, a key aspect of care management that should not be overlooked is the identification of resource shortfall. That is, where needs are identified but cannot be met through existing resources or a creative response, such information needs to be recorded and collated so that future social policy planning can be based on actual requirements, rather than distorted by a process that conceals or camouflages an inadequate level of resourcing.
- Underpinning all these aspects of good practice is the need to work within an anti-ageist framework. This involves focusing on empowerment, rather than routine service provision; recognizing the position of older people as a disadvantaged and oppressed group; and the need to avoid succumbing to ageist stereotypes.

Care management clearly involves an element of financial management and resource rationing, but to see the process solely or primarily in these terms is not only mistaken, but also dangerous. It represents a defeatist cynicism that is indulged in at the expense of vulnerable older people and their carers. It would clearly be naive to see care management as a panacea. However, the tendency, apparent in some quarters, to see care management as simply a thinly disguised exercise in cost-cutting represents an abandonment of the power practitioners have to capitalize on the benefits and minimize the tendency to reduce social work to an exercise in form-filling and accountancy.

In particular, a cynical approach to care management is dangerous insofar as it may distract attention away from important practice issues such as ensuring equality of opportunity. A negative and defeatist approach may not be sufficiently sensitive to the possibility of discrimination featuring in the processes of assessment, service provision and resource allocation. That is, an approach to community care that cannot look beyond the potential for care management becoming little more than a bureaucratic process is unlikely to be able to see, and respond to, the discrimination and oppression inherent in such a narrow focus. In short, if we do not seize upon the positive potential of care management, we shall be allowing the destructive, reductionist tendencies inherent in the process to hold sway.

Assessment

Assessment is a process closely associated with care management and community care. However, it is important to note that it can also be used in a much broader sense. For example, the first stage in any problem-solving process is likely to be an assessment – a gathering of information and the development of an action plan. We should be clear, then, that it is in this broader sense that I am using the term 'assessment' here. It extends far beyond the assessment of needs implicit in care management.

This is an important point to make, as assessment is a process that all staff working with older people are likely to be involved in at one time or another. Assessment is not simply an event that takes place when an older person first comes into contact with the health or welfare services. Assessment and reassessment are continuous processes, as circumstances continue to change and may therefore require new solutions or approaches.

Coulshed (1991) describes assessment in the following terms:

Assessment is an ongoing process, in which the client participates, whose purpose is to understand people in relation to their environment; it is a basis for planning what needs to be done to maintain, improve or bring about change in the person, the environment or both. The skill of undertaking and producing an assessment depends on administrative talent coupled with human relations skills. It takes someone who can organise, systematise and rationalise the knowledge gathered together with a gift of sensitivity in taking in the uniqueness of each person's situation. 'Hard' knowledge such as facts are pertinent, but so too are thoughts and feelings and the worker's own clarified intuition. (p. 24)

This is a very important passage as it encapsulates a number of key points, and each of these is worth highlighting:

- *An ongoing process*: This emphasizes the point already noted, that assessment is a process rather than an event.
- *Client participation*: Assessment is something we do *with* service users, rather than *to* them. The views, perspectives, values and preferences of the older person are an important element in developing a workable plan of action.
- *A basis for planning*: A common misunderstanding of assessment is that it is simply a process of gathering information. The reality is that the information gained is to serve as the basis of planning services or other forms of intervention. A mass of information on its own is of little value; it needs to be structured in such a way as to aid planning.
- *The person and the environment*: It has to be remembered that it is not the individual that is being assessed, but rather the situation, including the person and the environment in which he or she lives. Too narrow a focus on the individual can produce a tendency to be judgemental.
- *A range of skills*: Assessing involves a number of skills and, when practised well, amounts to a highly skilled activity. Indeed, a skilled intervention at the assessment stage can prevent the need for a great deal of intervention at a later stage (see the discussion of crisis intervention below).
- *Interpretation*: The information made available through assessment does not 'speak for itself'. It needs to be interpreted – processed in such a way that it presents an accurate, coherent picture that helps make sense of the situation.
- *Hard and soft information*: An assessment needs to be based, as far as possible, on facts rather than assumptions. However, what is also needed is the personal dimension. Assessment is an art as well as a science.

From a community care perspective, assessment is required to be needs-led, rather than service-led. That is, needs should be identified even if it is known that the services required to meet them are not available. In this way, service shortfall can be identified. However, this principle is not restricted to community care assessments. It has long been recognized as a principle of good practice that assessment should be holistic, that is, go beyond a simple attempt to slot people's needs into existing services. As Seed and Kaye (1994) comment: 'The idea of a needs-led assessment, then, was not invented with the National Health Service and Community Care Act 1990. But it was, in many ways, consolidated and the rhetoric gained a new prominence' (p. 25).

A service-led assessment also fails to take into consideration the strengths that older people and their carers bring to situations. A focus primarily on service availability distracts attention from the positives of a situation and the strong points that can be drawn upon to help resolve the problem identified. Such a focus also presents assessment as a precursor to service provision, rather than a broader part of any problem-solving process.

This issue is particularly significant when applied to working with older people. This is because of the pervasive role of ageism and its propensity to focus predominantly on negative aspects of old age, to portray older people in problematic terms, with little or no recognition of the strengths or positives of older people. In view of this, a narrow approach to assessment can be seen both to reflect and to reinforce ageist ideology.

A further danger associated with poor assessment practices is the mistake of seeking a solution before first defining the problem. This is often a response to pressure. Where a problem is quite pressing, perhaps very distressing, the temptation may be to go for a quick and easy solution when a closer examination of the circumstances causing concern is more likely to prove to be the wiser response. This is not to say that an urgent response is never appropriate, but it does underline the danger of acting prematurely and embarking on a course of action without first thinking it through.

Practice focus 5.2

Frank was a community psychiatric nurse (CPN) with many years' experience of working with older people. When he met Mr Kingsley he very soon formed a judgement that he was suffering from depression and set about organizing a programme of cognitive behavioural therapy. Frank had had a lot of success with this particular method in the past and was very surprised to find he made no headway with Mr Kingsley at all. The reason for this lack of success came to light while Frank was away on leave and Mr Kingsley was visited by Sandra, another CPN. What Sandra discovered, which Frank had not considered at all, was that Mr Kingsley was grieving the loss of a very close friend. Frank's haste to implement a solution before first undertaking a proper assessment of what needed to be done had therefore led him down the wrong alleyway.

Doel and Marsh (1992) follow a similar line of argument when they discuss the process of 'problem exploration':

> Problem exploration consists of an initial broad sketch followed by more detailed examination. The various problems need separating and then putting into some order so that the most important is evident and the whole picture makes sense for the client and the worker. A useful metaphor for this is the production of the *front page* of a newspaper. There are headlines and detailed stories, and the page layout needs deciding in the light of which story is to be the lead. (p. 25)

Counselling

The British Association for Counselling defines counselling in the following terms:

> Counselling is the skilled and principled use of a relationship to facilitate self-knowledge, emotional acceptance and growth, and the optimal development of personal resources. The overall aim is to provide an opportunity to work towards living more satisfyingly and resourcefully. Counselling relationships will vary according to need but may be concerned with developmental issues, addressing and resolving specific problems, making decisions, coping with crisis, developing personal insights and knowledge, working through feelings of inner conflict or improving relationships with others.
>
> The counsellor's role is to facilitate the client's work in ways that respect the client's values and personal resources and capacity for self determination. (BAC, 1989, p. 1, cited in Clarkson and Pokorny, 1994, p. 8)

Counselling, then, is more than 'having a chat', but differs from in-depth psychotherapy. Much of the work undertaken with older people therefore comes under the broad umbrella of counselling. This does not mean that every worker needs to be a trained counsellor. However, it does mean that a basic understanding of counselling can pay dividends by helping to offer more effective services.

A concept that appears frequently in the literature relating to counselling is that of loss. Loss is an experience that often brings with it a need for counselling. As we have already noted in Chapter 2, old age is a stage of life characterized by loss, indeed, often by multiple losses. The role of counselling in working with older people can therefore be seen to be potentially very significant.

In view of this, it is ironic that the use of counselling runs counter to the ageist notion that all that is needed in working with older people is 'common sense' and a caring approach. This irony is also reflected in the relative lack of literature relating to counselling older people. Scrutton

(1989) is one notable exception to this, and he makes apt comment when he asks:

> Is there an implicit assumption that old people do not require the development of 'theoretical constructs' such as counselling, that their needs are simple and can be accurately assessed and readily satisfied? Do we assume that age brings with it an easy ability to express personal feelings and needs? Or has the image of old age as a time of peace, tranquillity and serenity obscured the very real insecurities felt by many elderly people? (p. 9)

Ageism can therefore be a major barrier to the use of counselling. It can subtly dissuade us from bringing the benefits of counselling to distressed older people. Ageism can also act as a barrier in other ways:

- 'Unconditional positive regard' is a basic principle of counselling (Rogers, 1961) and implies that staff should not adopt a judgemental attitude. However, ageism, if not challenged, tends to produce just such an attitude.
- Counselling takes as a basic premise the belief that people can change if they so wish (Egan, 1994). Once again, ageist ideology conflicts with this by presenting older people in negative terms with little or no prospect of change.
- Internalized oppression, the subjective experience of ageism, can lead older people to reject counselling as they do not wish to 'be a nuisance'. That is, in devaluing themselves, they turn their backs on the value of a counselling relationship.

This introduces a further reason, then, why good practice needs to be anti-ageist practice. Unless we are conscious of the role of ageism in hampering the counselling process, our ability to produce positive results will be severely restricted.

If counselling can be undertaken from a perspective of anti-ageism, it can also be used as a means of countering ageism. As Scrutton (1989) comments: 'Counselling can be a valuable technique for combating the power of ageist attitudes' (p. 4). Counselling can help to unravel much of the socialization into negative expectations associated with ageism. Scrutton captures this point in the following passage:

> Every individual needs to feel a sense of personal worth. Everyone needs to have an identified social role. Everyone needs to have a realistic optimism regarding the future. For older people, each of these elements of self-image can be particularly difficult concepts to maintain and develop, for they are essentially optimistic factors which have to be applied to a stage in life popularly believed to possess little about which to be optimistic . . . Counselling has to 'de-condition' the way that older people look at themselves; they have to be encouraged to look

again at their supposed limitations and failings, and look more optimistically at what it is possible to achieve in old age. (1989, pp. 44–5)

Practice focus 5.3

Mr Jacobs had been a regular attender at the day centre over a period of years and so the staff were very surprised when he stopped attending. When June called on him to find out what lay behind his absence, she found him in very low spirits. He was adamant that he was not yet ready to return to the centre but welcomed the opportunity to talk about his feelings. From discussions with June it emerged that Mr Jacobs had developed a very negative outlook on his life and could only see the problems and limitations that faced him. However, through a process of brief counselling, June was able to help him develop a more balanced view by reappraising the positives in his life.

An important factor in developing an anti-ageist approach to counselling is the recognition of the problem of 'talking down' to older people. A propensity to address older people in patronizing terms (the use of the term 'dear', for example) stands in the way of a positive counselling relationship. A theoretical perspective that helps us make sense of this is transactional analysis, with its emphasis on the significance of inter-personal dynamics. Berne (1991) describes the three psychological states ('ego-states') of Parent, Adult and Child, and explains person-to-person interactions in terms of the interplay between these states. At its simplest, this means aiming for Adult-to-Adult interactions, rather than allowing one person to dominate another through a Parent-to-Child interaction (see Hough, 1994, for a helpful overview of this theory). Transactional analysis therefore gives us a model of counselling that can help us to guard against the dangers of infantilizing older people.

The development of counselling within a framework of anti-discriminatory practice is a relatively new undertaking, as McLeod (1993) acknowledges: 'On the whole, the theory and practice of counselling and psychotherapy have served the dominant groups in society and largely ignored the problems of people who are disadvantaged or discriminated against' (p. 108).

None the less, the positive value of counselling in working with older people makes the development of anti-ageist practice in this area a worthwhile investment of time and energy. One specific advantage of such a development is the potential for increased levels of trust as the barriers of ageism are brought down. Trust, as D.W. Johnson (1993) illustrates, is a basic ingredient of an effective counselling relationship:

> Trust is not a stable and unchanging personality trait. Trust is an aspect of relationships that constantly changes and varies. Everything individuals do increases or decreases the trust level in their relationship. The actions of both people are important in establishing and maintaining trust in their relationship. (p. 66)

Such trust is often a feature of day-to-day work, a common lubricant of everyday interactions. Indeed, this is an important point to emphasize with regard to counselling. As Scrutton (1989) acknowledges: 'Sensitive and caring people who are good listeners, who like people enough to allow them to express their feelings, are practising counselling' (p. 7). That is, counselling not only occurs at a formal, structured or planned level, it also occurs more informally between older people and a whole range of professional workers. However, as Scrutton notes:

> So while it is important to present counselling as a method that can be practised by any caring persons, it is also vital to stress that it is more than just 'being pleasant', more than just befriending, more than just 'talking to' people. Many people who do this may believe that they practise 'counselling', and have sound counselling relationships with older people, when in fact their role within the relationship is too dominant to be any such thing. (1989, p. 7)

Advocacy and mediation

Advocacy and mediation are two important roles often undertaken on behalf of older people. There is some degree of overlap between the two activities but also some significant differences. I shall concentrate primarily on advocacy but with some discussion of mediation later.

First, we need to be clear about what advocacy means. At a very basic level advocacy entails pleading a case on behalf of another person or group in order to obtain services or safeguard rights that would otherwise not be secured. It is therefore a process of representation.

Advocacy is commonly used in relation to welfare rights issues. It is not unusual for older people not to be claiming benefits to which they are entitled. The complexities of the benefits system, together with its reputation for not being user-friendly, often bring about a need for advocacy. It is therefore important that staff working with older people address issues, where appropriate, of benefit entitlement in order to help avoid the not uncommon situation of poverty being caused or exacerbated by an older person not finding his or her way successfully through the intricacies of the system.

Although much can be gained through the practice of advocacy, there are, however, also dangers associated with it. For example, the process can be misused by professionals to achieve their own objectives, and this can take precedence over the interests of the person being represented. Advocacy involves the exercise of power, and therefore introduces the possibility of the abuse of that power.

This possibility can be linked specifically to situations in which inadequate consultation has taken place, or in which communication has been of a poor standard. Advocacy entails representing the interests of another person or group, but 'representing' should not be equated with 'taking over'. Advocates often act from a position of expertise or specialist knowledge – the legal system or welfare rights, for example. None the less, a distinction has to be drawn between having expertise and being an expert if, by the latter, we mean 'someone who knows best'. In practising advocacy with older people, ageism increases the likelihood of this position being adopted. Consequently, it is essential that, wherever possible, full discussion takes place at every stage of the process in order to ensure that the advocate is not acting independently of the person's wishes.

A second danger is that the person acting as advocate can be affected by a conflict of interest. He or she may be in a position in which the interests of employing organization and service user are in conflict, and a situation of divided loyalties arises. One possible solution to this problem is the development of 'citizen advocacy'. This involves having volunteers who are trained in the skills and principles of advocacy. This gets round the problem of professional workers entering into a conflict of interest with their employers, who may be providing services, and thereby getting stuck in a 'Catch 22' situation.

A further potential danger is that of creating dependency. By acting on behalf of a person or group, we run the risk of taking away their motivation to solve their own problems. Twelvetrees (1991) comments on this in relation to advocacy with community groups:

> Acting as an advocate or broker has many dangers. The danger of making groups dependent on the worker is ever present; it is so often quicker for the worker to do the job herself, and the resulting outcome so obviously to the immediate benefit of the group, that 'product' can become more important than process. Yet the uniqueness of community development is that ordinary people can learn to do things for themselves. (p. 101)

The point that people can learn to do things for themselves is well made, although to describe this as unique to community development is clearly an exaggeration.

In undertaking advocacy work, care must therefore be taken to ensure that the net result is not that of dependency on the worker, but rather a step in the direction of empowerment – helping people gain control over their lives. An important strategy in this respect is the promotion, wherever possible, of 'self-advocacy'.

Bateman (1995) defines self-advocacy as: 'a process in which an individual, or a group of people, speak or act on their own behalf in pursuit of their own needs and interests' (p. 4). Staff working with older people can play an important role in encouraging and facilitating the development of self-advocacy. This can be achieved through:

- providing (or helping to seek out) the information or technical knowledge required to make a case;
- helping to clarify technical terminology so that language does not act as a barrier by mystifying the process;
- boosting confidence in whatever reasonable ways possible, helping to counteract the negative effects on self-esteem brought about by ageism;
- clarifying the process that is likely to occur by helping people to navigate their way through the system or systems concerned.

Advocacy is therefore a good example of the broader process of empowerment. A powerful group of people (staff) work positively with a relatively powerless group (older people) in order to help build up their power, influence and confidence.

One of the negative effects associated with ageism is the tendency to disregard the rights of older people, to play down their status as citizens (Thompson, 1992b). Advocacy, with its emphasis on rights and empowerment, therefore has an important part to play in anti-ageist practice. As Phillipson (1993b) comments:

> The general understanding of advocacy is that it is concerned with the balance of power between the client as a member of a minority or other disenfranchised group and the larger society. From the advocate's point of view, the client's problems are not seen as psychological or personal deficits but rather as stemming or arising from discrimination as regards social and economic opportunities. Therefore, techniques of intervention, rather than focusing solely on the relief of individual clients, should challenge those inequalities within the system which contribute to or cause difficulties for the older person. (pp. 182–3)

Closely linked to advocacy is the notion of mediation. The most significant difference between the two is that advocacy implies a degree of loyalty to the individual or group concerned, while mediation hinges on a

---

Practice focus 5.4

Mr Mahmoud lived in a flat above a newsagent's shop and, although it was not ideally suited to his needs due to the steep stairs, he was happy and settled there. However, when the newsagent's shop closed down, the landlord put great pressure on Mr Mahmoud to move out 'for his own good'. In actual fact, the landlord wanted to sell the property but knew that a sitting tenant could discourage potential buyers. When Mr Mahmoud explained the situation to his daughter, she enlisted the aid of a social worker who was able to marshal considerable support from Shelter in order to safeguard his rights as a tenant. The social worker and housing aid worker were able to act as advocates on behalf of Mr Mahmoud and help him put an end to the landlord's unfair (and illegal) pressure.

---

degree of neutrality. Mediation involves taking up a position of negotiator between two parties who are in conflict.

With older people, this role often applies where there is conflict between an older person and his or her carer(s). This can present the worker with a very sensitive and problematic situation. The needs and welfare of both parties have to be taken into consideration. This is for two separate, but related, reasons. First, although the older person is the primary client, carers are also clients. Second, if carers become alienated as a result of a conflict – or as a result of a mediator's mishandling of a conflict – this could cause a major problem for the older person.

The need for mediation may also arise between two or more older people, for example, in a residential setting or in a marital relationship. A significant danger in acting as a mediator in such situations is that of infantilization. For example, where a dispute occurs between two older people and leads to acrimonious exchanges between them, there may be a temptation to treat the two warring factions as 'naughty children', rather than adults who may need help in dealing with a difficult situation. Not unlike advocacy, mediation is a role fraught with difficulties and requiring considerable skill and sensitivity – but also a role of such potential that it repays the investment of time and energy required to become competent in these roles.

Creative methods

Working with older people has, unfortunately, tended not to be associated with creative methods or an imaginative approach. Of course, this is due, in no small part, to the influence of ageism. Indeed, ageism can be seen to discourage creativity in a number of ways:

- Older people are devalued, seen as unimportant, and therefore not worth the effort of developing a creative approach.
- Work with older people is commonly seen as routine and uninteresting, and is therefore unlikely to be associated with creativity.
- The dehumanization and depersonalization inherent in ageism lead to older people being categorized as 'all the same'. It is assumed that 'the elderly' have common needs and do not therefore require an imaginative or tailor-made approach.
- The assumed primary role in working with older people is to promote 'care'. If the focus is on 'looking after' older people, then a creative approach will be seen to have little value or applicability.

In adopting an anti-ageist perspective, we need to be wary of these tendencies to oversimplify a complex set of circumstances and simply see older people as a passive group of people who need to be 'looked after'. A broader focus on problem-solving, improving quality of life and promoting dignity offers a much less negative picture of working with older people, and one that is much more in touch with the complex and intricate realities of old age and the needs of older people. Furthermore, it will also offer a more creative approach that is not hidebound by routine or an uncritical 'tramlines' approach to practice.

Traditional approaches tend to close the door on important and valuable methods of intervention. Methods that are used extensively with other groups are far less likely to be used with older people, even though they may be equally applicable. Consider, for example, the case of crisis intervention. This is a method used a great deal in responding to mental health problems and, increasingly, in child care. Despite its success in these areas, it is, as I argued earlier, largely absent from work with older people.

A crisis is a turning point in a person's life, a time of 'make or break'. The positive intervention of a professional worker at, or soon after, this crucial time can make an immense difference in terms of bringing about beneficial change. It is therefore both an irony and a pity that crisis intervention is used relatively rarely with older people. This is particularly the case in view of the association between loss and crisis, and the number of losses associated with old age (as discussed in Chapter 2).

In much the same way as crisis intervention has been neglected, family work with older people has also received far less attention than it deserves. The significance of family issues has yet to be recognized by many people working with older people:

In many cases elderly clients live in families. This raises issues about family dynamics, power balances, communication and so on. If the family context is seen as vital in child care cases, why should it not be so where elderly people are concerned? Even where an elderly person does not live as part of a family, family issues can remain a significant influence. He or she will have grown up in a family and will have certain values associated with that family's style of functioning and characteristics. These may well have a bearing on the client's current situation. Ignoring the family context is hardly likely to contribute to good practice. (Thompson, 1989, p. ii)

Froggatt (1990) represents one of the few attempts to understand, and work with, older people from a family work perspective. She argues that:

Elderly people are almost always in some sense part of a family with kin-related and social support networks. Any change in the vulnerable elderly person's capacity to cope with daily living should be considered in relation to his/her place in the family network, and the capacity of that network to respond to the change. To that end, the development of a wider understanding of inter-generational relationships has been encouraged. One should also explore the present capacities of the client against the background of the life experience which shaped him/her. (p. 18)

It is important, then, that the narrow focus of traditional practice is not allowed to stand in the way of a more imaginative approach that incorporates methods of intervention which have demonstrated success with other client groups. Crisis intervention and family work have been used as examples, but many others have, potentially at least, something to offer. Indeed, this is the essence of a creative approach – being able and willing to go beyond the barriers of routine, convention and tradition.

However, there is more to a creative approach than broadening one's horizons by drawing on other methods, however wide their range. Henry (1991a) relates creativity to creating a fresh perspective and breaking away from old ideas. In this respect, creativity parallels the development of anti-ageist practice. Henry describes creativity in the following terms:

Creativity is about the quality of originality that leads to new ways of seeing and novel ideas. It is a thinking process associated with imagination, insight, invention, ingenuity, intuition, inspiration and illumination. However, creativity is not just about novelty: for an idea to be truly creative it must also be appropriate and useful. The related term innovation is usually used to describe the process whereby creative ideas are developed into something tangible, like a new product or practice. (p. 3)

Developing creativity is therefore quite a challenge, but is consistent with, rather than additional to, the challenge of developing anti-ageist practice. An approach to practice that encourages and facilitates creativity is therefore one that is very much to be appreciated and promoted.

Conclusion

Working with older people involves a wide range of tasks and duties, each with its own demands and challenges. Each can bring frustration or job satisfaction, or a mixture of both. Each can also play an important part in improving quality of life and promoting dignity. Equally, though, each can condone, reinforce or exacerbate the ageism to which older people are subject.

This places considerable pressure on us, as it means that mistakes can be quite costly. It reinforces the point that, if we are not part of the solution, we must be part of the problem. That is, the professional task plays a pivotal role, insofar as our practice can reflect ageism or counter it – there is no comfortable middle ground in which ageism is not an issue.

The discussions in this chapter have introduced a number of important issues that have a bearing on good practice. Simply exploring such issues will not, in itself, produce good practice, but can at least play a part in setting the scene for high-quality work for older people.

Many of the points raised here are relevant to working with people who have dementia. However, there are many more issues that need to be addressed in order to begin to understand anti-ageist practice in this complex and demanding area of work. It is for this reason that Chapter 6 is devoted to examining the challenge of dementia.

6 The challenge of dementia

Introduction

Dementia is a challenging condition for all concerned – the person with the illness, his or her carers and any health or social welfare staff who may be involved. However, many of the problems associated with dementia arise from misunderstandings and the fears that are often generated by them. This chapter therefore has two main aims. First, it seeks to provide a clear picture of dementia and some of the main issues, so that a number of fears and fallacies can be cleared away. Second, by promoting a better understanding of dementia, this chapter can lay the foundations for good practice in dealing with the demands and difficulties involved in meeting the challenge of dementia.

Before exploring a number of important issues, it is necessary to be clear about what is meant by the term 'dementia'. The first task, then, is to clarify what dementia is and, in so doing, be clear about what it is not.

What is dementia?

Dementia is often used loosely as a term to refer generally to the experience of confusion in old age. To use the term in this broad sense is both inaccurate and misleading. Victor (1991) offers a more precise understanding:

> Dementia may be defined as the global impairment of higher mental functioning including the loss of memory, problem solving ability, the use of learned skills and emotional control. The consciousness of the sufferer is not impaired. In

95

the most general of terms this condition is both progressive and irreversible. (pp. 66–7)

Whilst this positive definition of dementia is helpful, it is also necessary to tackle the question from a negative point of view; that is, to examine what dementia is not.

In order to distinguish dementia as it actually is from the popular misconceptions associated with it, I shall outline a number of ways in which other factors can be mistaken for dementia.

Normal ageing

A common misunderstanding is that dementia is an inevitable part of ageing that will apply to anyone who lives long enough to fall victim to it. This is reflected in the way the term 'senility', which literally means 'old age', has come to be used as a synonym for dementia. Dementia is a pathological condition, an illness, and is therefore by no means a normal aspect of ageing.

Acute confusional state

Dementia is characterized by an impaired level of mental functioning, what is commonly known as 'confusion'. However, confusion can also arise for a variety of other reasons. An 'acute confusional state', that is, a short-term experience of confusion of sudden onset, can be caused by a number of factors:

- A number of illnesses, particularly infections, can lead to confusion and disorientation.
- Physical injuries such as a blow to the head can also produce similar confusion.
- Reactions to medication can sometimes be of an adverse nature, including periods of confusion.
- Post-traumatic stress can also be a significant factor. That is, shock can temporarily produce symptoms similar to dementia.

Alcohol abuse

Excessive consumption of alcohol can have a negative effect on mental functioning. Where it is not apparent that such drinking is taking place, its effects may be mistaken for dementia. As Harvey (1990) comments:

Practice focus 6.1

Mrs Taylor was referred to Social Services by her GP, who believed she was in the early stages of dementia. He had referred her to the psychogeriatrician for confirmation of the diagnosis, while also requesting a social work assessment of the family's needs. The case was allocated to Neil, a social worker with a great deal of experience of working with people with dementia. On his first visit to the family, he began to take a social history. Mrs Taylor's two daughters were present but her son was not. Mention of her son visibly made the atmosphere very tense. In trying to find out why this was the case, Neil was clearly touching on a sore point. After further discussion it emerged that Mrs Taylor's son was in prison, having been convicted of a credit card fraud. This had had a profound effect on Mrs Taylor, and Neil began to suspect that this was a case of the effects of shock masquerading as symptoms of dementia. A week later, the psychogeriatrician visited and confirmed that Mrs Taylor was *not* suffering from dementia.

'Persistent drinking and the consequent mental deterioration can mimic dementia in the similarity of symptoms presented' (p. 9).

Depression

Depression can sometimes produce what is known as 'pseudodementia'. As Stuart-Hamilton (1994) comments:

> [Pseudodementia] can arise in elderly people who suffer severe depression . . . In becoming depressed, the old person loses motivation, and this is reflected in very poor scores on tests of mnemonic and other intellectual functions. This, and their general lack of interest in their surroundings, can provide an excellent impersonation of dementia (p. 146)

These examples make it clear that there is considerable scope for failing to distinguish between dementia and a number of other factors that can appear very similar. A major implication of this is that great care needs to be taken to ensure that we do not jump to conclusions by equating confusion in general with dementia in particular.

In terms of what dementia is not, it is also important to note that dementia is not a form of mental illness. Whether or not mental disorders such as schizophrenia or depression have a physical cause represents a fierce and long-standing debate, incorporating a wide variety of views on the subject. Dementia, by contrast, is not a subject of dispute. Its physical basis as an illness is fully demonstrated and widely accepted.

Types of dementia

The term dementia is a generic one. That is, it encapsulates a number of different conditions that share common characteristics. It is therefore important to develop an understanding, in broad outline at least, of the different types of dementia, as the differences may have implications for the type of care needed.

The most common type of dementia is Alzheimer's disease, as Hayslip and Panek (1993) comment:

> Alzheimer's is a disease of brain dysfunction named for its discoverer, Alois Alzheimer, in 1907. Many adults of normal intelligence become afflicted with Alzheimer's disease, which causes changes in their thinking and behaviour, from accustomed patterns to bizarre and disoriented confusion. Forty-five to 50 per cent of all dementias are due to Alzheimer's disease (Heston and White, 1991). (p. 404)

The second most common form of dementia is 'multi-infarct' dementia. Harvey (1990) describes it as follows:

> In this type of dementia, mental functioning is affected because oxygenated blood supplies to the brain are insufficient; therefore brain tissues die. The most likely medical explanation is hardening of the arteries. Individuals who have a history of arterial disorders, strokes or heart conditions are obviously more vulnerable to this type of dementia.
>
> Unlike Alzheimer's disease, the onset can be sudden and individuals can present with acute confusion, florid symptoms of memory loss and disorientation. Many appear to experience some recovery in their mental functioning until the next episode. People suffering with this kind of dementia often fluctuate in their mental functioning and personality changes are often less pronounced. (p. 15)

This passage helps to illustrate some of the ways in which the different types of dementia can lead to differences in care needs and related circumstances.

Alongside the two main types of dementia already outlined are a number of relatively rare forms of dementia. These include:

- Pick's disease;
- Huntington's chorea;
- Creutzfeldt-Jakob disease;
- Neurosyphilis.

It is also possible for other diseases, Parkinson's disease for example, to result in dementia.

As we have seen, Alzheimer's disease is by far the most prevalent type of dementia, although estimates as to the percentage of overall cases of dementia do tend to vary. There are also differences in the estimated prevalence of dementia in the elderly population, although Wattis and Martin's (1994) figures are not atypical: 'The overall prevalence rate for dementia in the over-65s is around ten per cent rising from two per cent of the 65–69 year age group to around 20 per cent of over-85 year old people' (p. 92).

Diagnosis and prognosis

The discussion earlier in this chapter of the possible mistakes in identifying dementia underlines the importance of a thorough and careful investigation before a diagnosis is confirmed. It is not surprising, then, that many GPs prefer to refer to a specialist, usually a psychogeriatrician, rather than frame their own diagnosis. Health and social welfare staff can play an important role in this by providing relevant information accurately and appropriately in order to assist the process of diagnosis. Diagnosis is more than a simple process of recognizing symptoms, and so the information provided by staff can be of great value.

In order to understand what information is relevant and helpful, a basic grasp of the symptoms of dementia is needed. Symptoms can be divided into two main types, physical and behavioural. The physical signs include:

- short-term memory loss;
- reduced mental functioning;
- incontinence.

However, what can be more noticeable, and more distressing, are the behavioural symptoms. These include:

- wandering;
- aggression;
- communication difficulties, including 'anomia', a failing ability to name objects;
- socially inappropriate behaviour;
- overactivity or obsessive behaviour.

These behavioural problems will be discussed below under the heading of 'The experience of dementia'.

A further important point to note in relation to the symptoms of dementia is that they tend to be different at different stages in the course of the illness. For example, incontinence is far more common in the later stages than the earlier ones. Similarly, short-term memory loss is common in the early stages but the loss of long-term memory can also occur in the final stages.

In addition to symptoms, another aspect to consider is that of risk factors. The extent to which the risk of developing dementia can be predicted remains poorly understood, although we do have some limited indications of potential risks. Victor (1991) summarizes the situation as follows:

> Establishing risk factors which identify those at an elevated risk of experiencing dementia is problematic because of multi-causality. It is probable that the risk factors for multi-infarct type are similar to those for stroke in which hypertension is implicated. To date there are few well established risk factors for dementia of the Alzheimer's disease type. Other interesting hypotheses about potential risk factors for dementia include educational status, ethnicity, Down's Syndrome, aluminium and a wide variety of social and environmental factors. (p. 83)

In terms of the prognosis for sufferers of dementia, it is important to stress that the illness is an irreversible degenerative one, with no known cure. That is, dementia is a terminal illness. This again underlines the need for appropriate diagnosis, as the implications of a diagnosis of dementia are, for all concerned, very profound.

The period of time between initial onset and death can vary considerably but tends to be between five and ten years. Arguably, very few people can be said to die of dementia itself. The reason for this is that, in the later stages, the sufferer is more vulnerable to other potentially fatal illnesses or strokes. It is therefore difficult for doctors to be precise in determining the actual cause of death.

Practice focus 6.2

Mrs Rees was very distressed when she learned that her mother was suffering from dementia, and did not want to talk about the matter. However, after a little while, she came to realize that she needed to be informed about the likely course of the disease. She therefore booked an appointment with the GP and went along armed with a list of questions to ask, including 'How will she die?' Dr Robson found this a very difficult question to answer but tried to explain that, in the later stages of the disease, her mother would become incapacitated and increasingly prone to potentially fatal infections, circulatory problems and so on. It would therefore be impossible to anticipate the likely cause of death. While this was not the type of answer Mrs Rees was looking for, this greater understanding of the disease did play a small part in helping her come to terms with the losses to come.

The experience of dementia

Dementia is an illness or, more accurately, a generic term for a collection of related illnesses. As such, there is a danger of focusing on the medical issues, the objective dimension, and neglecting the significance of the experience for those concerned, the subjective dimension. This section seeks to redress this imbalance to a certain extent by focusing on the experiential aspects of dementia for those concerned, particularly the problems encountered.

Dementia can be, and frequently is, a major source of pressure for carers; it can lead to considerable stress and the various problems associated with stress. Chapter 7 focuses on the experience of carers and the problems they encounter. In view of this, attention in this chapter will be concentrated mainly, albeit not exclusively, on the experience of the person with dementia.

In the case of Alzheimer's disease, onset tends to be gradual and can therefore lead to a number of problems and tensions. For example, forgetfulness can lead to family tensions when this occurs before a diagnosis is made, or even before illness is suspected. What are later understood to be symptoms of an illness may, at first, appear to be deliberate attempts to be awkward or uncooperative. In such situations, the older person concerned may not understand why their friends, neighbours or relatives are impatient, irritated or even hostile towards them. The result can be a very distressing, perhaps even frightening, experience.

Practice focus 6.3

Linda was a community nurse who visited Mrs Torrington to replace the dressings on her leg ulcers. On one particular occasion, she noticed the atmosphere in the family home was very tense indeed. When Linda commented on this, it appeared to open the floodgates as the family members poured forth a list of complaints about Mrs Torrington's 'awkwardness'. Linda had great difficulty getting them to be specific in detailing what the problems were. However, the situation continued to be very tense and it was only some months later, when a diagnosis of Alzheimer's disease was made, that Linda began to understand what had been at the root of the family turmoil.

Overall, dementia presents a range of problem situations and challenges. I shall consider, in turn, some of the main sets of difficulties experienced, although it is important to stress that the situations described here are possible outcomes, but are by no means inevitable.

Indecision

The reduced levels of mental functioning associated with dementia often result in a degree of indecisiveness. Even very simple decisions – whether to have tea or coffee, for example – can prove to be major hurdles and, in consequence, very distressing for all concerned.

From a practice point of view, it is important to recognize that there is a need to avoid the older person feeling pressurized. There is a danger that a vicious circle can develop in which pressure to make a decision can actually hinder the decision-making process further. There is therefore a need to find a balance whereby such decision-making problems are avoided as far as possible, but without taking away choice – and the dignity that goes with it.

Communication difficulties

Communication can be hampered in a number of ways. The person with dementia may:

- respond in a way which makes little or no sense;
- have a very short attention span;
- become almost totally withdrawn and uncommunicative;
- forget what has been said from one moment to the next.

Clearly, this can lead to a great deal of frustration. Again, there is a danger of a vicious circle arising. The frustration and tension caused by communication difficulties can make communication all the more difficult. A great deal of patience and sensitivity is therefore called for.

Wandering

Dementia often produces disorientation. That is, the person concerned can easily lose track of surroundings and forget where he or she is – even in very familiar surroundings. This can generate a significant amount of anxiety for carers and professional workers, particularly when there are major hazards nearby, such as busy roads, a river or canal, and so on.

Wandering can also occur within the home. A person with dementia may wander constantly around the home with no apparent purpose or reason. This can become a form of obsessive behaviour (see below) which can create a great deal of tension.

There is no guaranteed solution to this problem but two factors that experience suggests to be helpful are increased physical exercise and an emphasis on regular, stable routines. The former provides a degree of stimulation, the latter a degree of security.

Aggression

The subject of aggression was addressed more fully in Chapter 4 and so I shall not repeat those points here. However, it is important to note that aggression is often associated with dementia. A common explanation of this is in terms of the intense frustration that can be experienced as a result of the limitation imposed by the illness. However, what also needs to be considered is the breakdown of social inhibitions (see 'Inappropriate behaviour' below).

Incontinence

Once again, this is a problem that was addressed in Chapter 4. What can complicate the situation with regard to dementia are three specific factors:

- Anxiety and emotional trauma (Harvey, 1990), brought about by the experience of dementia, can increase the likelihood of incontinence occurring.
- Forgetfulness can present problems insofar as the route to the toilet may be forgotten, or the person may become distracted on the way.
- A loss of physical control, particularly in the later stages of the illness, can act as a barrier to achieving continence.

Incontinence seriously undermines dignity and therefore needs to be dealt with carefully and sensitively. I shall return to this point below when considering the principles of good practice.

Inappropriate behaviour

This can take a variety of forms but mainly encompassed by the following three categories:

- *Relaxation of social inhibitions*: When the rules of social behaviour are disregarded, major problems may arise. For example, the breakdown of sexual inhibitions can prove to be very embarrassing.
- *Obsessive behaviour*: Dementia can produce rigid, repetitive behaviour patterns that can prove very disruptive of social relationships. For

example, a person may repeatedly pick up a book, open it, close it and put it down again, thereby becoming a major source of irritation.

● *Hazardous behaviour*: This is a broad category that includes: not switching the cooker off after use, leaving items too close to a gas or electric fire, bathing or washing in scalding hot water, and so on. These behaviours can place the person at risk and can also generate considerable anxiety in carers and professional workers.

In dealing with these problems, it is important to avoid the danger of falling into the trap of infantilization, of treating the older person as a naughty child.

Memory loss

A decline in short-term memory can be seen as a significant factor in the behaviours outlined above, but can also be problematic in terms of:

● *Repetitive speech*: Constant repetition can occur because, once a sentence is uttered, the person may forget that it has been said, and therefore feels the need to say it again, and so on indefinitely.
● *Dressing*: A person with dementia may have difficulty dressing, not for reasons of physical incapacity, but due to a failure of memory, in terms of what items to wear and how to put them on.
● *Hygiene*: There may be a tendency to neglect personal hygiene (washing, cleaning teeth and so on) as well as household hygiene (cleanliness, flushing the toilet and so on).
● *Misplacing items*: The misplacing of important items such as a purse or pension book can lead to false recriminations against carers. The loss of an item can be falsely equated with theft, and this is likely to result in ill-feeling and resentment.

There may also be difficulties with regard to disorientation of time. That is, night-time can be confused with daytime and inappropriate activities may result (for example, going to the shops at 3 a.m.). The problems associated with memory loss can cause a great deal of frustration, and so there is a danger that this can spill over into anger or even hostility. Patience and calm are therefore important qualities to develop.

Loss and change

Gardner (1993) makes the important point that:

The word dementia is almost interchangeable with the word loss. The disease process is about a gradual loss in functioning and the deterioration of a person's personality. The loss of your very being must be the most significant loss that anyone can suffer. For the carer, as well as the person with dementia, there are many losses. The worker can assist in identifying and articulating these losses. It is important to investigate what other losses the client has had in their life and how they dealt with them. A loss now can trigger the feelings associated with previous losses and how previous losses were dealt with will determine the client's preferred way of dealing with this loss. (p. 31)

This situation presents a number of challenges for workers and adds weight to the point made in Chapter 2 that old age is characterized by loss.

Principles of good practice

Dementia, as we have seen, raises a number of demands. It is, therefore, all the more important that we develop good practice, so that we are as well-equipped as possible to make a positive contribution to quality of life. The final section of this chapter is therefore devoted to outlining what can be identified as the principles of good practice in meeting the challenge of dementia.

Establish a diagnosis

The point has already been made that a medical diagnosis is needed before assumptions are made about the reasons for a person's confusion or other apparent symptoms of dementia. It is important that the term dementia should not be used loosely as a synonym for confusion. Dementia is an irreversible, terminal illness and so a premature assumption that dementia is present can lead to a great deal of unnecessary grief and anxiety.

Clearly, it is not the task of social or health care workers to *make* a diagnosis, but there is an important role in establishing a diagnosis by seeking the involvement of an appropriate medical practitioner.

Focus on the person

Dementia can leave the person concerned as a mere shadow of his or her former self. It is as if the person has died but the body continues to exist (a point to which I shall return in Chapter 7). Kitwood (1993) argues that a 'technical' approach to dementia that focuses on the illness can contribute to losing sight of the person, seeing the illness but not the individual. He comments on a more positive approach that focuses on the person:

When dementia is framed in a way that puts personhood at the centre, a rich and challenging agenda is set for care-giving. The prime task is that of doing positive 'person-work', so as to enable the dementia sufferer to be and remain a full participant in our shared humanity. (pp. 104–5)

He goes on to describe three ways in which this can be promoted:

One aspect of this work is 'validation': actively acknowledging the reality and subjective truth of the dementia sufferer's frame of reference (Feil, 1982). Another aspect is 'holding': providing a safe space when emotions such as fear, rage and grief can be experienced and worked through. Another is 'facilitation': filling out gestures or part-actions so that they become completed social acts . . . Increasingly, then, it is being realised that a purely technical frame has had its day. (p. 105)

Practice focus 6.4

Pat had relatively little experience of working with people with dementia but was keen to do a good job and had read extensively on the subject. She knew, for example, of the dangers of dehumanizing older people through a 'technical frame of reference'. One day, in conversation with Mrs Green, who had dementia, a problem arose when Mrs Green's niece began to dominate the conversation and speak about her aunt as if she were not there. Pat felt very uncomfortable about this and made the point, tactfully but firmly, that she did not think it appropriate to talk about Mrs Green as if she were not able to understand, thereby depersonalizing her. At this point, Mrs Green, who had very limited speech capability, grabbed Pat's arm, squeezed it tight and nodded and smiled approvingly. This helped to illustrate vividly Pat's point that we should not lose sight of the *person*.

Unconditional positive regard

This is a concept that was introduced in Chapter 5, and refers to the need to avoid adopting a judgemental attitude. It also applies to working with people with dementia with regard to the frustration that can build up. The pressures of this type of work can, at times, be difficult to bear. Considerable tension and frustration can be experienced which can, in turn, manifest themselves as a resentful, uncaring or even hostile attitude or approach. Unconditional positive regard involves not allowing one's own sense of frustration to stand in the way of good practice.

This indicates the need to develop strategies for coping so that (legitimate) negative feelings are not allowed to spill over into unprofessional behaviour in which we take out our frustrations on the person with dementia, or his or her carers. Effective supervision and other opportunities for support are an important part of this (Morrison, 1993).

Environmental change

Many of the problems encountered by people with dementia and their carers can be resolved or alleviated by changes or adjustments to the environment in which they live. In particular, hazards can be removed or lessened so that risk, and the anxiety that goes with it, can be diminished. For example, replacing a traditional kettle heated on a gas cooker with an electric kettle with an automatic shut-off can take away a fire risk.

In Chapter 5, the importance and value of a creative approach was stressed. Looking for environmental improvements is an area of practice in which a creative approach can come into its own. An imaginative outlook can pay dividends in finding solutions to problems and making improvements to quality of life. Encouraging creative thinking and developing powers of imagination are therefore important strategies for meeting the challenge of dementia.

Finding a way around problems

Many of the problems associated with dementia are intractable. That is, they are problems that cannot be solved, but may be alleviated or avoided. In general terms, it is not advisable to fail to confront problems, as they have a habit of getting worse if not addressed. However, where a problem is intractable (due to memory loss, for example) a better strategy may be to avoid the problem, rather than tackle it head on. For example, where a person engages in repetitive or obsessive behaviour, trying to deal with the problem directly is unlikely to be effective, and may actually make the situation worse. However, a strategy of distracting the person can be far more successful. Similarly, increased levels of physical exercise and mental stimulation can prove very helpful, even though they do not address the behaviour directly.

Assessment

The importance of diagnosis has already been emphasized. However, diagnosis is no substitute for assessment. Assessment is an essential precursor to intervention, a basic plan that presents an overview of the situation, the issues to be tackled and possible ways forward. As Gardner (1993) comments:

> When assessing individuals, couples, families or groups where dementia is present it is important to get a total picture of the functioning, both present and past. It is essential, however, to investigate the following:
>
> - medical assessment of person with dementia
> - family and social networks
> - life cycle stage of all concerned
> - social and economic situation
> - previous ways of dealing with a crisis
> - perceptions of the problem
> - what has brought them to seek help at this time
> - current functioning of all concerned. (p. 19)

Time devoted to assessment is therefore an important investment and should prove beneficial in terms of a better understanding of the situation and a clearer picture of what needs to be done.

Acknowledging the family context

In Chapter 5, the point was made that the family context of an older person is often neglected and its significance not fully appreciated. The same point can usefully be restated with regard to the circumstances of people with dementia. As Sherlock and Gardner (1993) comment: 'Dementia is an illness which generally impacts on the whole family and it is therefore valuable for workers in this field to develop skills in intervening with the family as a unit' (p. 63).

Illnesses in general can have a profound impact on family dynamics but dementia can go far beyond this and be extremely powerful in its influence on family relationships, expectations and practices. Indeed, it can be very destructive of families.

Multidisciplinary approaches

Dementia is a multifaceted entity. It creates a wide range of demands and calls for a variety of skills and responses. No single professional can encompass all that is required to meet the needs of a person with dementia and his or her carers. This introduces the need for a multidisciplinary approach.

Where a number of people work together, there is scope for wasteful overlapping, significant gaps in provision, misunderstanding and even open conflict. Good practice therefore needs to be based on a co-ordinated, multidisciplinary approach that rises above interprofessional rivalry and succeeds in placing the service user's needs first.

Valuing the past

Reality orientation is a therapeutic technique that can help confused older people retain a firmer grip on where they are or what time of day it is through a process of repeated reminders and other forms of stimulation. A related technique is that of reminiscence therapy. This involves positively valuing the past and drawing on the distinct psychological benefits of a process of life review.

Coleman (1994) comments on four important points in relation to reminiscence therapy. These are:

- *Finding positive memories*: This technique allows a deliberate focus on positive memories.
- *Confronting painful memories*: A sensitive approach to painful memories can help to create 'rounded life-stories, and the creativity and sense of fulfilment this promotes' (p. 18).
- *Empowering memories inhibited by grief*: The experience of grief can act as a barrier to the positive benefits of reminiscence. Effective grief work may therefore be a necessary precursor to life review.
- *Encouraging non-narcissistic memories*: The use of reminiscence can be a boost to the individual's self-esteem, but if this becomes self-indulgent, it can be a source of irritation to others and cause tension and conflict.

Overall, then, positively valuing the past has much to commend it as a therapeutic tool, but it needs to be used sensitively and purposefully (Bender, 1993; Gibson, 1993).

Avoid destructive processes

A major focus throughout this book has been the need to develop anti-ageist practice. This is particularly important in relation to working with people with dementia for, as we have seen, there is a strong tendency towards dehumanization. There are, however, a number of other destructive processes that need to be avoided if anti-ageist practice is to develop. Kitwood (1993) provides a list of such processes and it is worth quoting it in full:

> *Treachery*: the use of dishonest representation or deception in order to obtain compliance.

Disempowerment: doing for a dementia sufferer what he or she can in fact do, albeit clumsily or slowly.

Infantilisation: implying that a dementia sufferer has the mentality or capability of a baby or young child.

Condemnation: blaming; the attribution of malicious or seditious motives, especially when the dementia sufferer is distressed.

Intimidation: the use of threats, commands or physical assault; the abuse of power.

Stigmatisation: turning a dementia sufferer into an alien, a diseased object, an outcast, especially through verbal labels.

Outpacing: the delivery of information or instruction at a rate far beyond that which can be processed.

Invalidation: the ignoring or discounting of a dementia sufferer's subjective states – especially feelings of distress or bewilderment.

Banishment: the removal of a dementia sufferer from the human milieu, either physically or psychologically.

Objectification: treating a person like a lump of dead matter; to be measured, pushed around, drained, filled, polished, dumped, etc. (p. 104)

Clearly, none of the items on this list has a place within an anti-ageist framework, except as processes to be avoided, challenged and undermined.

Conclusion

For staff in health and social welfare, dementia is a difficult and demanding aspect of the work, a source of considerable pressure and a wide range of problems. However, with these challenges come opportunities for playing a very positive role in the life of a person with dementia and, potentially at least, gaining immense job satisfaction in the process, a justified reward for the major investment of time, energy and emotional resources that is necessary to undertake this type of work successfully.

One particularly significant aspect of working with people with dementia that can offer considerable scope for success is in the support of carers. Indeed, in working with older people in general, the role of informal carers is a crucial one that merits close attention. It is for this reason that Chapter 7 is devoted to 'caring for the carers'.

7 Caring for the carers

Introduction

The implementation of the NHS and Community Care Act 1990 has brought into sharp focus the dividing line between state-provided services and those from the private and voluntary sectors. However, what much of this debate takes for granted is the huge amount of support for older people – practical, emotional and financial support – provided by informal carers. As Smale *et al.* (1993) comment:

> In Britain there are some 6 million unpaid carers of people other than children, of whom 1.4 million devote over twenty hours per week to caring, and a quarter have looked after a dependent person for at least ten years. Nearly two thirds of carers, 3.7 million, carry the main responsibility for a dependent person, either alone or jointly with someone else, and so act as a 'care manager' as well as direct service provider. (p. 24)

Friends, relatives and neighbours therefore form a very significant group of people. Consequently, the quality of life of very many older people depends very heavily on this important group of people.

Many carers face considerable demands and immense pressures as a result of their caring role. In view of this, the question of 'caring for the carers' arises. What steps can be taken to support carers, both for their own sake and the sake of the people they care for? This chapter therefore addresses this question and raises a number of important issues relating to the role of carers in promoting dignity and quality of life.

Who are the carers?

An important concept in relation to this question is that of 'the double equation of community care', a notion strongly associated with Finch andGroves (1983). Community care is basically equated with care by the family, and care by the family is primarily equated with care by women. The first point to note concerning carers, then, is that they are predominantly women. As Qureshi and Walker (1986) comment: 'Within the family it is female kin who are by far and away the main providers of care' (p. 15).

Dalley (1993) takes this point a step further and comments on the close links between women and caring:

> Women have a very real and legitimate interest in the whole issue of caring. First, there is an ideology of caring which has underpinned many of the social forms of care which prevail today: it is one which favours women's leading role and the pre-eminence of family-based models of care. Second, there is enough persuasive evidence to show that women have and still do bear the greater burden of care although clearly men have a part to play. Third, there is evidence that women themselves are the largest recipients of care once they reach old age. Thus, at certain stages of their lives women provide care, often at considerable cost to themselves and, at a later stage, they are often the people in most need of care. (p. 106)

Gender is therefore a significant dimension of informal care for older people, and so a sensitivity to gender and the dangers of sexism is an important element of good practice in caring for the carers.

A further aspect to be considered is that of the age of carers. Daughters and daughters-in-law are frequently the carers of older people. But, if those being cared for are in their 80s, their carers are likely to be in their 60s. To use Marshall's (1990) terminology, 'old old' people are being looked after by 'young old' people:

> The newly retired are often the people who care for their older relatives. Many 90 year olds are cared for by children in their 60s and 70s. Sometimes this care imposes an incredible strain. The strain can be physical and help needs to be organised for jobs like bathing, dressing and bedmaking. Sometimes the strain is emotional. People can be trapped at home with a mentally or physically frail relative and they may need a sitting service or respite breaks when their relative goes into some sort of care. Sometimes it is a question of money, and often these people could have claimed extra financial help like attendance allowance had they known about it. (pp. 20–1)

The pressures of caring

The role of carer is one characterized by a range of pressures that can add up to a considerable degree of strain. It has to be recognized that caring for an elderly person can be very stressful and carries with it a number ofpersonal costs. This can particularly be the case when it is a person with dementia who is being cared for. As Stuart-Hamilton (1994) comments: 'There is ample evidence that caring for a demented relative usually results in significantly higher levels of depression, stress and other related health problems' (p. 164).

As was noted in Chapter 4, the pressures on carers can be a contributory factor in elder abuse, part of the process of reaching the end of one's tether. This is by no means the only factor in the development of abusive situations, but does play a part. The pressures of caring may produce a situation in which essential caring tasks are not carried out (resulting in neglect) or are carried out in a mechanical, unfeeling way (resulting in emotional, or even physical, abuse). Jerrome (1993) refers to the work of Wenger (1987) and reiterates her argument that:

> Taking a life-span approach helps us to appreciate the personal significance of family transactions and reminds us of something we often forget: that the act of caring means caring *about* as well as caring *for* . . . This approach also puts the concept of filial maturity – the coming to terms with a parent's dependence – into perspective. It is not to deny, however, that very occasionally caring *for* takes place in the absence of caring about. We are reminded by a growing literature on the abuse of elderly people by their families that negative feelings may dominate a care relationship with harmful consequences. (p. 195)

A parallel distinction can be drawn between caring and tending. 'Caring' describes the emotional response or attitude, whilst 'tending' refers to the

---

Practice focus 7.1

Mrs Griffiths had been caring for her mother for nearly five years. During that time her mother had become increasingly dependent on her for physical care due to her arthritis, rheumatism and, of late, incontinence. There had been little support from the statutory or voluntary services and she had struggled on almost totally alone in her caring role. Mrs Griffiths had never complained about undertaking these tasks but now, after so long without a life of her own, she was carrying them out on 'automatic pilot'. She went about her business in an almost mechanical way, with no thought or feeling going into it. She was indeed 'tending' her mother but any actual caring had now been completely drained from her.

physical tasks of caring. Where tending takes place without caring, abuse becomes a possibility.

This is not to say that excessive pressures turn caring people into uncaring abusers overnight. However, exposure to sustained high levels of pressure can lead to uncharacteristic behaviours. Eastman (1994), describing the findings of an American study, comments that:

> Significantly, the abuse was not triggered by any one event but came about as a result of a deterioration in the relationship between an increasingly dependent elderly person and a 'carer' who was, in many cases, unequal to, or unprepared for, the work. (p. 28)

However, strain on carers arises not simply from the amount of pressure, but also from the nature of such pressures. This applies in a number of ways:

- *Guilt*: Adopting a major caring role involves a number of losses. And, as the literature on loss consistently argues (Worden, 1991), guilt is a feeling strongly associated with loss. It is not surprising, then, that carers feel guilty, despite the absence of a rational basis for such feelings. Guilt can be a source of pressure in itself, but can also make other pressures more difficult to bear, as it tends to undermine coping skills.

- *Helplessness*: This too is a feeling associated with loss, but is also engendered by feeling trapped in the caring role. The demands of the situation may be such that carers feel they have no way out of what increasingly comes to be seen as a trap. One consequence of this is a sense of helplessness, a feeling that nothing can be done to help. At this point the carer can abandon hope and plunge into depression.

- *A restricted life-world*: A major involvement in caring tends to have a significant impact on personal and social experiences – it restricts carers in terms of employment opportunities, friendships and social activities, hobbies or interests. In short, it makes it difficult for carers to feel they have a significant source of pressure in its own right but also has the effect of undermining coping skills.

- *Intergenerational conflicts*: In old age the traditional pattern of parents caring for their children is often reversed. This can produce intergenerational conflicts. Hocking (1994) provides one example of this when she comments that: 'If children were brought up strictly, with high expectations but distant love, they may in turn wish to punish their elderly parents for embarrassing, socially unacceptable behaviour' (p. 53).

- *Lack of recognition*: Smale *et al.* (1993) point out that carers often feel abandoned and unsupported. Their efforts frequently go unrecognized, unappreciated and unrewarded. However, for those caring for someone with dementia, there is another form of lack of recognition that can prove to be very stressful. As the Alzheimer's Disease Society (1993) comment:

> One of the cruellest aspects of Alzheimer's disease, and that which is cited by carers as the most emotionally draining, is the fact that many people with dementia no longer recognise the person who is caring for them.
> Husbands and wives, in particular, describe the distress caused by caring for a much loved spouse who doesn't know them any more or, even worse, who regards them as an enemy to be feared and blamed. (p. 6)

This is not an exhaustive list of the types of pressure that carers can and do face, but it does begin to paint a picture of the difficulties associated with the role of carer. It helps to emphasize the need to take seriously the needs of carers and recognize the dangers of leaving carers unsupported. Carers' needs and strategies for supporting carers are therefore important issues to be addressed.

The needs of carers

The King's Fund Centre produces a very helpful leaflet entitled *Carers' Needs: A Ten Point Plan for Carers*, and I shall use its ten-point structure as a basis for this section of the chapter.

It is important to acknowledge that carers need:

1 *Recognition of their contribution and of their own needs as individuals in their own right.*

The caring role can be, as I have already noted, a very unrewarding one, and carers can feel that they are not valued – by the person being cared for, by other family members, by professionals or by wider society.

This sense of not being valued tends to have a detrimental effect on self-esteem and can therefore leave the carer more vulnerable to depression and less well-equipped to deal with the stresses associated with caring. A lack of recognition of the carer's own needs can be seen to have an insidious effect insofar as it tends to undermine the individual's sense of self. A carer's identity can be overwhelmed by the dominance of the caring role which expands to take up a major proportion of the carer's thoughts, feelings, time and energy.

2 *Services tailored to their individual circumstances, needs and views, through discussions at the time help is being planned.*

One aspect of ageist practice is the use of routine, generalized responses to situations in place of individualized plans and interventions. This too can be seen to apply to carers if individual circumstances and needs are not taken into consideration. This reflects the ageist process of dehumanization, a denial of individual humanity.

Similarly, anti-ageist practice entails working in partnership with older people, rather than excluding them from decision-making and planning. The same logic can be seen to apply to carers. In order to be empowered they need to be consulted and involved at every stage.

3   *Services which reflect an awareness of differing racial, cultural and religious backgrounds and values, equally accessible to carers of every race and ethnic origin.*

Carers from ethnic minorities face racism in addition to the pressures of caring, and so it is important that services not only avoid exacerbating racism but also go some way towards challenging it. For example, if racism features in the allocation of scarce resources, black carers will be significantly disadvantaged by this.

Similarly, services need to be ethnically sensitive by respecting cultural needs, values and practices. If, for example, an older person attends a day centre where culturally inappropriate food is all that is available, the benefits of respite for the carer may well be outweighed by the problems caused.

4   *Opportunities for a break, both for short spells (an afternoon) and for long periods (a week or more), to relax and have time to themselves.*

Respite care can be a great relief for over-burdened carers. This can work in two ways: the actual break from caring tasks and responsibilities can be very helpful in itself as and when it occurs; and, knowing that a break is due to occur at a specified date in the future can give something to look forward to, an important part of maintaining a life for oneself.

However, as with other forms of help, respite care should not be used indiscriminately. It needs to be used as part of an overall plan and care package. For example, feelings of guilt or difficulties in adjusting to having time to oneself can prevent a carer from taking full advantage of a respite opportunity. It may be necessary to work with the carer to ensure, as far as possible, that the service is used to maximum benefit.

5   *Practical help to lighten the tasks of caring, including domestic help, home adaptations, incontinence services and help with transport.*

The carer has a primary role in helping the older person maintain dignity and as much quality of life as possible. In turn, professional workers, and the services they represent, have a major role in maintaining the dignity and quality of life of the carer. This needs to be facilitated through taking the necessary steps to ensure a supportive environment and the services needed to maintain it.

This fits neatly with the care management role. A needs-led assessment lays the foundation for a package of measures designed to support the older person and his or her carers in whatever ways are necessary. Clearly, there will be financial limitations on the services provided but, as I argued in Chapter 5, implicit in the care manager role is the identification of service shortfall to inform future planning.

6   *Someone to talk to about their own emotional needs, at the outset of caring, while they are caring and when the caring task is over.*

As Qureshi and Walker (1986) comment: 'we do not want to lose sight of the fact that care comprises a social relationship as well as a physical task' (p. 6). The demands of caring are personal and emotional, as well as physical. This introduces the need to discuss experiences, express feelings and feel reassured that someone is concerned for their welfare and is prepared to listen to their concerns. This can be achieved on a one-to-one basis or through group support, or a mixture of the two.

This can have important benefits in the early stages when adjusting to the caring role, on an ongoing basis and, finally, when caring comes to an end and emotions can be running very high.

7   *Information about available benefits and services as well as how to cope with the particular condition of the person cared for.*

Information is a source of power and therefore a basis of empowerment. Without the appropriate information and understanding, carers will be handicapped in carrying out their tasks. There is, therefore, a need to make sure that the necessary information is available, that carers are not hampered from having access to it and are not afraid to use it.

The information may need to be explained, or put into context. Similarly, its implications may need to be drawn out. This identifies an educational role in supporting carers to deal with the pressures they face. This is a point to which I shall return below.

8   *An income which covers the cost of caring and which does not preclude carers taking employment or sharing care with other people.*

This is partly linked to point No. 7 in terms of the provision of information, particularly welfare benefits information. Each year large sums of money go unclaimed by potential benefit claimants due, in no small part, to a lack of awareness of what is available and how to claim it.

However, providing the necessary information to allow benefits to be claimed is not the only task that can usefully be accomplished. As noted in Chapter 5, advocacy can be an important function for workers to fulfil. Information is often not enough to guide carers through the complex web of the benefits system and the barriers that can stand in the way of successful claims.

9   *Opportunities to explore alternatives to family care, both for the immediate and long-term future.*

The dominant view that families should care for their elders can leave carers feeling that residential care, even on a short-term basis, amounts to a failure of duty. This sense of failure can produce considerable guilt and therefore act as a major barrier to considering alternatives to family care. It has to be recognized that carers have limitations in terms of the amount of care they can provide and the period of time over which they can provide it.

In view of this, it is important that professional workers do not reinforce this sense of failure or guilt by trying to discourage carers from considering alternatives to family care.

10   *Services designed through consultation with carers, at all levels of policy planning.*

The point has already been made that good practice is premised on involving carers by working in partnership with them. This principle then needs to be extended to apply more broadly to the policy process. That is, consultation is valuable not only at the point of delivery of services, but also in the various stages of planning that precede and underpin such services.

Carers bring an important perspective to the planning process and have a significant contribution to make. Of equal importance, carers also have a right to be heard.

Supporting carers

Caring, as we have seen, is a highly pressurized activity and potentially very stressful. Consequently the question of support becomes a very important one to address:

Much of the traditional literature on stress ignores or marginalises the question of support. Stress management is seen as a set of techniques for steeling oneself against occupational and life stresses. (Thompson *et al.*, 1994, p. 31)

A narrow view of stress has a tendency to 'blame the victim', to see him or her as lacking in the necessary resilience to cope with the pressures encountered. The experience of stress becomes equated with a failure on the part of individuals to deal with the demands made upon them. This is a harsh view which fails to take account of the vitally important role of support.

Practice focus 7.2

Sarah Forbes and Tracey Lee took over the care of their grandmother when their mother died. They were very anxious about the pressures they now faced, especially as they were still feeling very weak and vulnerable after the loss of their mother. At first, they turned down all offers of help, as they felt it was their duty to sort out the caring arrangements between them. However, as the pressures began to wear them down, they reconsidered the offers of help and decided to accept them. Very soon they were receiving support and the psychological effect of knowing they were not alone was a major boost to their coping abilities.

In working with carers there is a danger that we can take for granted their resilience and robustness, and therefore fail to consider the positive benefits of support and the damage that can be done by failing to provide such support when required. There is, therefore, much to be gained by exploring the ways in which supports of various kinds can usefully be provided for carers.

The issues covered here by no means form a comprehensive list but do provide an overview of a range of steps that can be taken to ensure that the notion of 'caring for the carers' becomes more than rhetoric. I shall present the strategies under five headings, the final one of which addresses empowerment and therefore receives a more in-depth treatment than the others in view of its central role in anti-ageist practice.

The educational role

A number of problems experienced by carers can be seen to derive from a lack of understanding of the ageing process and related issues. For example, a great deal of anxiety and tension can be generated by carers expecting an older person to eat a great deal, and then becoming worried when he or she eats relatively little. This is a common source of difficulties in relationships but can be rectified fairly easily by helping carers understand that the energy requirements of a relatively inactive older person can be quite meagre. This basic understanding and reassurance can go a long way towards defusing tense situations and creating a more positive atmosphere. As in so many other life situations, a small misunderstanding can produce a major problem or level of difficulty.

The worker's knowledge of the various aspects of the ageing process (see Chapter 2), together with his or her experience of working with a wide variety of carers across a range of situations, can play an extremely valuable role in helping carers deal with difficulties. This educational role can be achieved on a one-to-one basis alongside other interactions with carers, or it can be achieved through support group activity (see below).

Positive strokes

This is another example of how a little positive intervention can go a long way. The pressures of caring can, as we have noted, produce feelings of helplessness and being trapped. These, in turn, can have a detrimental effect on self-esteem and self-image, thus producing a negative outlook or set of attitudes. Some degree of reassurance, together with positive strokes in relation to the important caring work done, can pay dividends in helping carers feel valued, appreciated and thus motivated and able to gain some satisfaction from their work.

Ironically, many people seem to find it difficult to give positive strokes. They feel uncomfortable in giving praise or expressing positive comments about the quality or extent of work achieved. Workers who feel this way therefore have to face the challenge of overcoming this reluctance to give positive strokes, as the immense value of positive feedback is far too important to be allowed to go to waste.

Respite

The question of respite care was introduced earlier under the heading of 'The needs of carers'. It is an important issue that merits closer attention. It can be an essential source of relief for heavily burdened carers but can also be counterproductive, both for the carer and the older person concerned.

Problems associated with respite care include:

- guilt on the part of the carer;
- anxiety and disorientation on the part of the older person;
- a lack of availability or flexibility (George, 1994).

Practice focus 7.3

Chris was a home care organizer who regularly came into contact with carers. She tried very hard to be supportive of carers but had not given any thought to the question of 'positive strokes'. However, one day she attended a workshop as part of a training course and was involved in discussion of the importance of positive feedback. This made a big impact on Chris as she was able to see the constructive potential of using positive strokes where appropriate. She therefore decided to make this an aspect of her own practice in working with carers. She very soon came to realize that she had made the right decision as her use of positive feedback very quickly began to pay dividends.

Perhaps the most significant problem is the danger of respite care being used routinely and uncritically, a 'standard' solution to a 'standard' problem. When respite is used sensitively as part of a well-thought-out plan, its value can be considerable and, in many cases, it is the vital ingredient that prevents the care situation breaking down.

Counselling

In Chapter 5 the value of counselling for older people was emphasized. The same argument can now be applied to carers. Having the opportunity to discuss the caring situation and the feelings it generates can be an invaluable resource for carers. Sustained high levels of pressure can cause a distortion of one's sense of perspective – it can be difficult to keep things in proportion. Counselling offers the potential to regain a sense of perspective and maintain as much control as possible over the situation.

However, one danger associated with counselling is that it may come to be seen as a sign of weakness in the individual, an indication of his or her inadequacy in dealing with pressures (Thompson *et al.*, 1994). It is therefore important that counselling is not presented in this light, and that such a conception of counselling is challenged when or if it is encountered.

Counselling, if used appropriately, can make a big difference to the experience of the caring role. For example, Totman (1990) comments on the value of 'attribution therapies':

Attribution therapists use a variety of techniques to replace attitudes of helplessness and negativity with attitudes of effectiveness – in particular, the attitude that one has control over one's own life. This is referred to by various names, 'personal control training', 'assertiveness training', 'social skills training', 'cognitive restructuring', and so forth. The essence of these therapies is that someone (the therapist) injects meaning into someone else's (the client's) life using professional techniques to change attitudes about the self. (p. 174)

Empowerment

This is a central role for all staff working with older people and involves facilitating as much control as possible for the individual over his or her life and circumstances. This is vitally important for maintaining dignity and promoting anti-ageist practice.

Empowerment is a broad process that encompasses a wide range of activities and issues. Consequently, it can be made a reality in a number of different ways. That is, there is no single, uniform means of empowering carers, but rather a wide variety of potential strategies, some of which are outlined here.

One aspect of good practice that has already received attention in this book is that of adjusting the home environment in ways that reduce difficulties and enhance coping. This can also be seen to apply to the situations faced by carers. For example, an elderly person who is prone to falling may be helped by having the furniture rearranged so that it provides something to hold on to along the route. This can reduce the need for supervision by the carer and contribute to a lower level of anxiety and concern.

In this way, a 'user-friendly' home environment can remove a lot of restrictions on carers and provide a degree of freedom and control that would otherwise be denied them. As discussed in Chapter 5, workers can play a significant role in facilitating environmental changes that ease the pressures of caring. Such changes are often expensive, such as adaptations to buildings, and require applications for grant funding. Frequently, however, the changes to be made can be effected at little or no cost. A sensitivity to the potential for environmental improvement offers opportunities for creating positive changes that can be of major benefit to carers, and the people they care for.

Such a sensitivity forms the basis of a pragmatic approach that can generate creative solutions. Indeed, this in itself can be a source of empowerment, insofar as a focus on practical advice and imaginative responses to the difficulties encountered can help carers deal positively with the problems and demands of the caring role. Looking for practical and creative solutions is directly useful but also has the indirect benefit of allowing carers the reassurance of knowing that someone else shares their concerns and has a commitment to dealing with them. This can prove to have a very powerful positive impact. It helps to create a genuine partnership and move away from paternalism. It is this sense of partnership, of shared ownership, that can make such a difference in promoting empowerment.

Partnership as a basis for empowerment also manifests itself in terms of the participation of carers in planning and reviewing services. As was noted earlier, involvement at this level is recognized as something that carers need. It now also needs to be recognized that such participation is an additional important source of empowerment insofar as it offers a greater degree of control and influence and, furthermore, helps to value, and validate, the caring role.

A further major means of promoting empowerment is the use of groupwork. By bringing carers together to share perceptions and discuss common experience, considerable benefits can be attained. In particular, Mullender and Ward (1991) link groupwork with empowerment, and point out the positive potential of groups for countering oppression. Groupwork can play a part in empowering carers through a variety of means:

- producing a sense of solidarity and sharing which helps to combat feelings of isolation and helplessness;
- providing opportunities for the ventilation of feelings and scope for mutual reassurance;
- exploring avenues for mutual support, for example sitting services;
- sharing ideas and suggestions for problem-solving;
- providing opportunities for socializing and relaxation;
- giving access to wider support networks.

Setting up, facilitating and servicing support groups for carers are therefore important and worthwhile activities for professional workers to undertake.

A central theme underpinning the process of empowerment is that of confidence. Without some degree of confidence, carers will be unable to

---

Practice focus 7.4

Dot was the manager of a resource centre for older people. In providing respite services at the centre, Dot was well aware of the range of pressures carers faced and felt that more needed to be done to help them. Consequently, she arranged to set up a support group for carers. At first, she needed to be actively involved in facilitating the group but, as the group became more established and the carers became more confident, she was able to withdraw. She was delighted that she had succeeded in empowering the group and was already considering setting up a second group.

take maximum advantage of opportunities to take control of their lives and pursue their own direction. If carers are to feel they have a life of their own and are not entirely governed by forces beyond their control, then confidence is likely to play a central role.

In view of this, a sensitivity to issues of confidence can be seen to be an essential part of the professional worker's repertoire. Without this, there is not only the danger that valuable opportunities for boosting confidence will be wasted, but also the possibility that fragile confidence will be undermined by insensitive comments or actions. In this respect, confidence is very like trust – it takes a long time to establish firmly, but can easily be destroyed in a short period of time.

Empowerment, it could reasonably be argued, is a central part of good practice in health and social welfare. However, in the case of working with the carers of older people, its significance is particularly heightened. This is because, as we have seen, carers as a group are more likely to feel trapped and powerless, robbed of individual identity and a life of their own. On this basis, empowerment emerges as a vital ingredient of potential solutions to the complex problems of supporting carers.

Conclusion

Many of the older people in receipt of health or social welfare services have no one to care for them and this very fact is often a significant factor in the reasons for such services being needed. But there are also very many older people who do have carers, predominantly family members such as daughters or daughters-in-law. Such carers, as we have seen, play a vital role in making community care a reality above and beyond rhetorical policy statements.

Without the commitment, energy and effort of carers, there could be no community care. The combined efforts of the public, voluntary and private sectors would be doomed to failure if they were not so well supported by so many unpaid carers who are prepared to devote considerable time and effort, often at great personal cost to themselves, to the health and well-being of another person or persons.

In this chapter we have begun to unravel some of the key implications of this situation. I have highlighted a number of important points that have a significant bearing on the quality of work with older people and, indeed, with their carers. These key issues include:

- Carers are predominantly women and are often of retirement age themselves.

- Caring brings with it a number of pressures and these can amount to an immense source of stress.
- Sometimes the nature or extent of pressure can be a significant factor in the development of abusive situations.
- Carers have a number of needs that are often overlooked or paid inadequate attention.
- Carers can be supported by professional workers in a number of ways, including education, positive strokes, respite, counselling and various forms of empowerment.
- Empowerment is a central issue of primary importance and a fundamental part of anti-ageist practice.

There remains much to be learned in terms of how best we can 'care for the carers', but the points raised and issues discussed in this chapter can take us at least some way towards a better understanding of what is needed to promote good practice in working with carers.

If older people are to be empowered and treated with dignity, then so too must their carers. To leave carers feeling vulnerable, unsupported and without a life of their own is not only oppressive in its own right, but also seriously weakens the anti-ageist project insofar as it significantly undermines an important resource upon whom so many older people rely.

8 Conclusion: Developing anti-ageist practice

In terms of health and welfare practice, older people are playing an increasingly significant part due to the demographic changes that are leading to higher numbers of people in old age. The need to look carefully at good practice is being intensified by these changes. However, regardless of the demographic factors, good practice in working with older people is a subject worthy of attention in its own right. For so long older people's needs have tended to be a low priority and have often been neglected to quite an unacceptable extent. Unless these issues are firmly and clearly on the agenda, work with older people will continue to be marginalized, under-resourced and undervalued.

It was primarily for this reason that the book began with a chapter addressing the significance of ageism and arguing the case for the development of anti-ageist practice. Unless these issues are explicitly addressed, the dominance of ageist actions, attitudes and structures will continue to flourish in an atmosphere in which older people are rarely, if ever, accorded the respect, dignity and full human status to which they are entitled.

Such ageism is also reflected in much of the literature on the ageing process insofar as it tends to focus primarily, if not exclusively, on the biological aspects of ageing. By failing to examine the other dimensions of ageing – psychological, social, political and philosophical, for example – traditional accounts of the ageing process present a distorted, one-sided view of old age. This view then adds fuel to the fire of ageism by presenting a narrow, depersonalized perspective with unduly negative connotations that reinforce destructive ageist stereotypes. Chapter 2 therefore played an important role in challenging ageism by questioning the narrowness of traditional views and by reasserting the significance of the other dimensions so often neglected.

Chapter 3 also reflected the theme of ageism by outlining key elements of law and policy relating to older people and identifying the potential for oppression inherent in so many aspects of the policy context. Balanced against this was the highlighting of opportunities within the current legal and policy framework for promoting anti-ageist practice. As is the case with law and policy generally, dominant norms will reflect dominant (ageist) ideas and values, but will also present opportunities for countering, challenging and undermining such dominant norms.

Old age brings with it its own problems, as indeed does any stage of the life course, but these are exacerbated and multiplied by the fact that we live and work in an ageist society, a society that assigns its older citizens to a lower status, a form of underclass. The range of problems older people potentially face is therefore not insignificant. While Chapter 4 outlined many of these problems and their implications, Chapter 5 complemented this by examining the professional task, the range of tasks and duties undertaken by staff working with older people. Understanding this range can not only enhance one's own level of practice, but also improve interprofessional co-operation by helping each worker to begin to appreciate the pressures and demands faced by other workers within a multidisciplinary network.

Occupying a central position in the range of problems workers encounter, dementia places both informal carers and paid workers under immense pressure in addition to being a source of great distress to the person with the disease. Unfortunately, the difficulties brought about by the different types of dementia are once again exacerbated by ageism. For example, the dehumanizing tendencies of ageism combine with the loss of personality associated with dementia to produce situations in which the individual is almost totally depersonalized.

This is only one of the many destructive processes engendered by the onset and course of dementia. Chapter 6 outlined a number of questions posed by the challenge of dementia, including the demands on carers. This set the scene for Chapter 7 in which the question of caring for the carers was addressed more broadly. What emerged clearly from this chapter was the enormity of the task faced by so many carers and the pressing need for professional workers to play an active and constructive part in supporting carers as fully as possible. In particular, the importance of empowering carers was stressed so that they could gain as much control as possible over the pressurized lives they lead.

This, then, brings us up to the present chapter, and here the aim is to draw the book to a conclusion by summarizing the key themes of anti-ageist practice that have underpinned the discussions throughout. This is to be achieved through sketching out what could be termed a charter for anti-ageist practice. This takes the form of two lists, a set of *dos* and *don'ts* that capture the basic principles of good practice as informed by a commitment to anti-ageism. These lists are partly informed by my previous published work on this subject (Thompson, 1992b, 1993) which, in turn, was informed by a number of published sources, my own extensive experience as a practitioner and discussions with students, colleagues and practitioners over a number of years. I shall begin with the list of things to avoid, the *don'ts*:

- *Don't* treat people as things (dehumanization). The tendency to deny older people their full humanity is a strong one and manifests itself in a number of ways. A common example of this is the denial of sexuality in old age.
- *Don't* leave older people out (marginalization). Dominant social expectations place older people on the margins of society, rather than within the mainstream. It is important that our actions and attitudes at a micro level do not reinforce this tendency at a macro level.
- *Don't* deny rights. This is often done in a spirit of seeking to safeguard a person from risk (Thompson, 1992b). However, the negative impact of being denied one's rights (and the dignity that goes with them) can so easily outweigh the benefits of being protected from a particular risk or set of risks.
- *Don't* stereotype. Stereotyping is a destructive process that denies individuality and identity. In particular, stereotypes of older people tend to be very negative and demeaning, a reflection of ageist ideology.
- *Don't* regard old age as an illness (medicalization). A common (false) assumption is that older people are necessarily frail and in need of medical attention or supervision. This 'broad brush' approach is a highly problematic one as it undermines confidence and coping resources.
- *Don't* create dependency. Some people may get a feeling of being valued when someone is dependent upon them. However, this is at the cost of disempowering the person concerned. Sometimes a degree of dependency is inevitable but it is not something to be encouraged.
- *Don't* ignore social divisions. Older people are not only subject to ageism. Other forms of oppression such as sexism, racism and disablism also affect groups of older people. Efforts to challenge ageism need to go hand in hand with other aspects of anti-discriminatory practice.
- *Don't* treat older people as children (infantilization). As we saw in Chapter 1, older people are often treated as children, as if they have gone beyond adulthood into 'postadulthood', and thereby lost their status as full citizens. Care must therefore be taken to ensure that all interactions take place on an adult-to-adult basis.

- *Don't* take carers for granted. Community care relies heavily on the goodwill, commitment and hard work of unpaid carers. It is therefore important that professional workers do not devalue carers by taking them for granted.
- *Don't* ignore death. Loss and death are significant in all stages of the life course but have a particular relevance for old age. The tendency to turn our back on death and pretend it is not an issue is therefore not a helpful basis for working with older people.
- *Don't* get stuck in routines. Good practice with older people requires vision, imagination and creativity in order to make the best use of limited resources in difficult circumstances. Getting stuck in routine forms of practice is therefore counterproductive.
- *Don't* collude with ageism. Countering ageism is a major undertaking due to the deeply ingrained nature of structures, attitudes and practices. At times, the struggle can seem too much and we become prone to defeatism, feeling that we can achieve little or nothing. When this occurs, there is a danger that we indirectly condone ageism and thereby collude with it. In this way, we switch from being part of the solution to being part of the problem.

These are some of the many destructive actions, attitudes and processes that need to be avoided in the development of anti-ageist practice. In addition to these, there are a number of positive, proactive steps that can be taken. These include:

- *Do* encourage participation and involvement. Working in partnership should apply at all levels, from direct practice to service planning. Excluding older people only serves to underline and exacerbate marginalization.
- *Do* promote interdependency. We all rely on other people in one way or another and so the importance of interdependency needs to be recognized. This is a much more constructive notion than the one-way dependency that some traditional forms of practice tend to foster.
- *Do* challenge ageism. Avoiding ageism in one's own work is a necessary part of good practice. However, this also needs to be supplemented by a willingness to challenge ageism in others or in organizational practices and structures.
- *Do* engage with the person. One aspect of bad practice with distinctly ageist overtones is the tendency to deal with older people in a mechanical, unfeeling way without engaging with the person at all. Care therefore needs to be taken to ensure that we communicate and interact as person to person.

- *Do* adopt a holistic perspective. There is a danger that, in dealing with people who may be frail or dependent in some particular way, we may see only the frailty or the dependency. Other aspects of the person can become submerged unless we recognize the need for a holistic perspective.
- *Do* be sensitive to language. The words we use in our day-to-day language carry with them significant overtones. That is, an uncritical use of language can contribute to patronizing, demeaning, marginalizing and dehumanizing older people. Forms of language more consistent with dignity and respect are called for.
- *Do* assess and reassess. Dealing with older people in a routine, uncritical way leaves little or no room for assessment. Problems are seen in standardized ways, and this removes the need to produce tailor-made solutions. Assessment is therefore needed to make sure that such an inappropriate blanket approach is not adopted.
- *Do* promote empowerment. It has consistently been argued that the process of empowering older people – helping them gain more control over their life and circumstances – is a central feature of anti-ageist practice. It acts as an essential means of countering the destructive processes associated with ageism.

No list of practical guidelines can ensure anti-ageist practice. A commitment to promoting dignity for older people entails a commitment to recognizing, challenging and undermining ageism. Practical guidelines can assist or facilitate putting this commitment into practice, but what they cannot do is act as a substitute for such commitment. It follows, then, that the suggestions presented here are not rules to be followed slavishly or mechanistically. They are intended as pointers to stimulate developments in practice that run counter to ageist discrimination and oppression. They are, then, part of the solution but are not sufficient in themselves to guarantee that work with older people is characterized by dignity, and is free from negative stereotypes. We can, however, draw strength from the fact that, by striving towards anti-ageist practice, we are making a contribution towards a positive experience of old age.

References

Adelman, M. (1990) 'Stigma, Gay Lifestyles and Adjustment to Aging: A Study of Later-life Gay Men and Lesbians', *Journal of Homosexuality* 20.

Ahmad, B. (1990) *Black Perspectives in Social Work*, Birmingham: Venture Press.

Ahmad-Aziz, A., Froggatt, A., Richardson, T., Whittaker, T. and Leung, T. (1992) *Anti-Racist Social Work Education: Improving Practice with Elders*, London: CCETSW.

Alzheimer's Disease Society (1993) *Deprivation and Dementia*, London: Alzheimer's Disease Society.

Arber, S. and Evandrou, M. (eds) (1993) *Ageing, Independence and the Life Course*, London: Jessica Kingsley.

BAC (1989) *Invitation to Membership* (Form No. 1, Oct.), Rugby: British Association for Counselling.

Ball, C. (1992) *Law for Social Workers: An Introduction*, 2nd edn, London: Blackstone Press.

Barclay, P. (1982) *Social Workers: Their Role and Tasks*, London: Bedford Square Press.

Bateman, N. (1995) *Advocacy Skills*, Aldershot: Arena.

Beauvoir, S. de (1972) *The Second Sex*, Harmondsworth: Penguin.

Beauvoir, S. de (1977) *Old Age*, Harmondsworth: Penguin.

Bee, H.L. and Mitchell, S.L. (1980) *The Developing Person*, London: Harper and Row.

Bender, M. (1993) 'An Interesting Confusion: What Can We Do with Reminiscence Groupwork?', in Bornat (1994).

Bennett, G. and Ebrahim, S. (1992) *The Essentials of Health Care of the Elderly*, London: Edward Arnold.

Bennett, G. and Kingston, P. (1993) *Elder Abuse: Concepts, Theories and Interventions*, London: Chapman and Hall.

Bennett, K.C. and Thompson, N.L. (1990) 'Accelerated Aging and Male Homosexuality: Australian Evidence in A Continuing Debate', *Journal of Homosexuality* 20.

Bernard, M. and Meade, K. (1993a) 'Perspectives on the Lives of Older Women', in Bernard and Meade (1993b).

Bernard, M. and Meade, K. (eds) (1993b) *Women Come of Age: Perspectives on the Lives of Older People*, London: Edward Arnold.

Berne, E. (1991) *Transactional Analysis in Psychotherapy*, London: Souvenir Press.

Beveridge, W. (1942) *Social Insurance and Allied Services*, London: HMSO.

Biggs, S.J. (1993) *Understanding Ageing*, Buckingham: Open University Press.

Biggs, S.J. and Phillipson, C. (1994) 'Elder Abuse and Neglect: Developing Training Programmes', in Eastman (1994).

Blakemore, K. and Boneham, M. (1994) *Age, Race and Ethnicity: A Comparative Approach*, Buckingham: Open University Press.

Board for Social Responsibility (1990) *Ageing*, London: Church House Publishing.

Bond, J., Coleman, P. and Peace, S. (eds) (1993) *Ageing in Society*, 2nd edn, London: Sage.

Bornat, J. (ed.) (1994) *Reminiscence Reviewed: Perspectives, Evaluations, Achievements*, Buckingham: Open University Press.

Boud, D., Cohen, R. and Walker, D. (1993) *Using Experience for Learning*, Buckingham: Open University Press.

Braye, S. and Preston-Shoot, M. (1992) *Practising Social Work Law*, London: Macmillan.

Brayne, H. and Martin, G. (1993) *Law for Social Workers*, 3rd edn, London: Blackstone Press.

Buckle, J. (1981) *Intake Teams*, London: Tavistock.

Byrne, T. and Padfield, C. (1985) *Social Services Made Simple*, London: Heinemann.

Bytheway, B. and Johnson, J. (1990) 'On Defining Ageism', *Critical Social Policy* 29.

Carter, P., Jeffs, T. and Smith, M. (eds) (1989) *Yearbook of Social Work and Social Welfare* 1, Milton Keynes: Open University Press.

Carver, V. and Liddiard, P. (eds) (1978) *An Ageing Population*, Sevenoaks: Hodder and Stoughton.

Cattell, R.B. (1971) *Abilities: Their Structure, Growth and Action*, Boston: Houghton Mifflin.

Chakrabarti, M. (1990) *Racial Prejudice*, Milton Keynes: Open University, Workbook 6, K254 Working with Children and Young People.

Chapman, A. and Marshall, M. (eds) (1993) *Dementia: New Skills for Social Workers*, London: Jessica Kingsley.

Clarkson, P. and Pokorny, M. (1994) *The Handbook of Psychotherapy*, London: Routledge.

Coleman, P. (1993) 'Psychological Ageing', in Bond *et al.* (1993).

Coleman, P. (1994) 'Reminiscence Within the Study of Ageing', in Bornat (1994).

Coulshed, V. (1991) *Social Work Practice: An Introduction*, 2nd edn, London: Macmillan.

CPA (1990) *Community Life: A Code of Practice for Community Care*, London: Centre for Policy on Ageing.

CRE/ADSS (1978) *Multi-Racial Britain: Social Services Department Responses*, London: CRE/ADSS.

Cumming, E. and Henry, W.E. (1961) *Growing Old*, New York: Basic Books.

Dalley, G. (1993) 'Caring: A Legitimate Interest of Older Women', in Bernard and Meade (1993b).

Davis, K. (1986) 'DISABILITY and the BOMB – The Connection', Clay Cross: Derbyshire Coalition of Disabled People.

Department of Health and Welsh Office (1990) *Mental Health Act 1983: Code of Practice*, London: HMSO.

Doel, M. and Marsh, P. (1992) *Task-Centred Social Work*, Aldershot: Ashgate.

Doka, K. and Morgan, J.D. (eds) (1993) *Death and Spirituality*, Amityville, NY: Baywood.

Eastman, M. (ed.) (1994) *Old Age Abuse: A New Perspective*, London: Chapman and Hall.

Edelman, M. (1987) *Constructing the Political Spectacle*, Chicago: University of Chicago Press.

Egan, G. (1994) *The Skilled Helper*, 5th edn, Pacific Grove, CA: Brooks/Cole.

Encyclopaedia Britannica (1990) 5th edn.

Feil, N. (1982) *Validation: The Feil Method*, Cleveland, OH: Edward Feil Productions.

Fennell, G., Phillipson, C. and Evers, H. (1988) *The Sociology of Old Age*, Milton Keynes: Open University Press.

Finch, J. and Groves, D. (eds) (1983) *A Labour of Love*, London: Routledge & Kegan Paul.

Finkelstein, V. (1981) *Disability and Professional Attitudes*, Sevenoaks: NAIDEX Convention.

Fishwick, C. (1992) *Community Care and Control*, Birmingham: Pepar.

Ford, J. and Sinclair, R. (1989) 'Women's Experience of Old Age', in Carter *et al.* (1989).

Froggatt, A. (1990) *Family Work with Elderly People*, London: Macmillan.

Gardner, I. (1993) 'Psychotherapeutic Interventions with Individuals and Families Where Dementia is Present', in Chapman and Marshall (1993).

George, J. (1994) 'Racial Aspects of Elder Abuse', in Eastman (1994).

Gibson, F. (1993) 'The Use of the Past', in Chapman and Marshall (1993).

Gibson, H.B. (1992) *The Emotional and Sexual Lives of Older People*, London: Chapman and Hall.

Gilleard, C. (1994) 'Physical Abuse in Homes and Hospitals', in Eastman (1994).

GLC (1985) *Changing the World: A London Charter for Lesbian and Gay Rights*, London: Greater London Council.

Graebner, W. (1980) *A History of Retirement: The Meaning and Function of an American Institution, 1885–1978*, New Haven, CT: Yale University Press.

Griffiths, R. (1988) *Community Care: An Agenda for Action*, London: HMSO.

Gross, R.D. (1992) *Psychology: The Science of Mind and Behaviour*, 2nd edn, London: Hodder & Stoughton.

Harvey, M. (1990) *Who's Confused?*, Birmingham: Pepar.

Hayes, N. (1994) *Foundations of Psychology: An Introductory Text*, London: Routledge.

Hayslip, B. and Panek, P.E. (1993) *Adult Development and Aging*, 2nd edn, New York: HarperCollins.

Henry, J. (1991a) 'Making Sense of Creativity', in Henry (1991b).

Henry, J. (ed.) (1991b) *Creative Management*, London: Sage.

Henwood, M. (1993) 'Age Discrimination in Health Care', in Johnson and Slater (1993).

Heston, L.L. and White, J.A. (1991) *The Vanishing Mind*, New York: Freeman.

Hill, M. (1988) *Understanding Social Policy*, 3rd edn, Oxford: Basil Blackwell.

Hockey, J. and James, A. (1993) *Growing Up and Growing Old*, London: Sage.

Hocking, E. (1994) 'Caring for Carers: Understanding the Process that Leads to Abuse', in Eastman (1994).

Hough, M. (1994) *A Practical Approach to Counselling*, London: Pitman.

Hughes, B. and Mtezuka, M. (1992) 'Social Work and Older Women: Where Have Older Women Gone?', in Langan and Day (1992).

Hulley, T. and Clarke, J. (1991) 'Social Problems: Social Construction and Social Causation', in Loney *et al.* (1991).

Jack, R. (1994) 'Dependence, Power and Violation: Gender Issues in Abuse of Elderly People by Formal Carers', in Eastman (1994).

Jerrome, D. (1993) 'Intimate Relationships', in Bond *et al.* (1993).

Johnson, D.W. (1993) *Reaching Out: Interpersonal Effectiveness and Self-Actualization*, 5th edn, London: Allyn and Bacon.

Johnson, J. (1993) 'Does Group Living Work?', in Johnson and Slater (1993).

Johnson, J. and Slater, R. (eds) (1993) *Ageing and Later Life*, London: Sage.

Johnson, M.L. (1976) 'That Was Your Life: A Biographical Approach to Later Life', in Munnichs and Van den Heuval (1976).

Johnson, N. (1987) *The Welfare State in Transition*, Brighton: Wheatsheaf.

Johnson, N. (1990) *Reconstructing the Welfare State*, Hemel Hempstead: Harvester Wheatsheaf.

Kitwood, T. (1993) 'Frames of Reference for an Understanding of Dementia', in Johnson and Slater (1993).

Kosberg, J. (ed.) (1983) *Abuse and the Maltreatment of the Elderly – Causes and Interventions*, Boston, MA: John Wright.

Langan, M. and Day, L. (eds) (1992) *Women, Oppression and Social Work*, London: Routledge.

Langan, M. and Lee, P. (eds) (1989) *Radical Social Work Today*, London: Unwin Hyman.

Leonard, P. (1984) *Personality and Ideology*, London: Macmillan.

Loney, M., Bocock, R., Clarke, J., Cochrane, A., Graham, P. and Wilson, M. (eds) (1991) *The State or the Market: Politics and Welfare in Contemporary Britain*, 2nd edn, London: Sage.

McCreadie, C. (1994) 'Introduction: The Issues, Practice and Policy', in Eastman (1994).

McDonald, M. and Taylor, M. (1993) *Elders and the Law*, Birmingham: Pepar.

McLeod, J. (1993) *An Introduction to Counselling*, Buckingham: Open University Press.

Marshall, M. (1990) *Social Work with Old People*, 2nd edn, London: Macmillan.

Midwinter, E. (1990) 'An Ageing World: The Equivocal Response', *Ageing and Society* 10.

More, W.S. (1990) *Aggression and Violence*, Birmingham: Pepar.

Morgan, J.K. (1993) 'The Existential Quest for Meaning', in Doka and Morgan (1993).

Morrison, T. (1993) *Staff Supervision in Social Care*, London: Longman.

Moss, M.S. and Moss, S.Z. (1993) 'Anticipation of the Death of an Elderly Parent', Paper presented at the Ethical Issues in the Care of the Aged, the Dying and the Bereaved conference, London, Ontario, Canada, May.

Mullender, A. and Ward, A. (1991) *Self-Directed Groupwork: Users Take Action for Empowerment*, London: Whiting and Birch.

Munnichs, J.M.A. and Van den Heuval, W.J.A. (1976) *Dependency or Interdependency in Old Age*, The Hague: Martinus Nijhoff.

Murphy, E. (1993) 'Depression in Later Life', in Johnson and Slater (1993).

Musgrove, F. (1964) *Youth and the Social Order*, London: Routledge.

Norman, A. (1985) *Growing Old in a Second Homeland*, London: Centre for Policy on Ageing.

Oliver, M. (1983) *Social Work with Disabled People*, London: Macmillan.

Oliver, M. (1990) *The Politics of Disablement*, London: Macmillan.

Orme, J. and Glastonbury, B. (1993) *Care Management*, London: Macmillan.

Patel, N. (1990) *A Race Against Time*, London: Runnymede Trust.

Peace, S. (1986) 'The Forgotten Female: Social Policy and Older Women', in Phillipson and Walker (1986).

Phillipson, C. (1982) *Capitalism and the Construction of Old Age*, London: Macmillan.

Phillipson, C. (1989) 'Challenging Dependency: Towards a New Social Work with Older People', in Langan and Lee (1989).

Phillipson, C. (1993a) 'The Sociology of Retirement', in Bond *et al.* (1993).

Phillipson, C. (1993b) 'Approaches to Advocacy', in Johnson and Slater (1993).

Phillipson, C. and Walker, A. (eds) (1986) *Ageing and Social Policy: A Critical Assessment*, Aldershot: Gower.

Picton, G. (1991) 'The Social Context Of Ageing', in Shaw (1991).

Postman, N. (1983) *The Disappearance of Childhood*, London: W.H. Allen.

Pugh, R. (1994) 'Language Policy and Social Work', *Social Work* 39(4).

Pugh, R. (1996) *Effective Language for Health and Social Work: Closing the Gap*, London: Chapman & Hall.

Punnett, R. (1976) *British Government and Politics*, London: Heinemann.

Qureshi, H. and Walker, A. (1986) 'Caring for Elderly People: The Family and the State', in Phillipson and Walker (1986).

Ratna, L. (1990) 'Crisis Intervention: Where it is Contraindicated', Paper presented at the First International Conference on Crisis Intervention Approach in Mental Health, London, May.

Rogers, C. (1961) *On Becoming a Person*, London: Constable.

Rooney, B. (1987) *Racism and Resistance to Change*, Liverpool: Merseyside Area Profile Group.

Samson, C. (1994) 'The Three Faces of Privatisation', *Sociology* 28(1).

Scrutton, S. (1989) *Counselling Older People*, London: Edward Arnold.

Seed, P. and Kaye, G. (1994) *Handbook for Assessing and Managing Care in the Community*, London: Jessica Kingsley.

Shaw, M.W. (ed.) (1991) *The Challenge of Ageing*, 2nd edn, London: Churchill Livingstone.

Sherlock, J. and Gardner, I. (1993) 'Systemic Family Intervention', in Chapman and Marshall (1993).

Sidell, M. (1993) 'Death, Dying and Bereavement', in Bond *et al.* (1993).

Smale, G., Tuson, G. with Biehal, N. (1993) *Empowerment, Assessment, Care Management and The Skilled Worker*, London: HMSO.

Solomon, K. (1983) 'Victimization by Health Professionals and the Psychologic Response of the Elderly', in Kosberg (1983).

Sontag, S. (1978) 'The Double Standard of Ageing', in Carver and Liddiard (1978).

Stainton Rogers, W. and Stainton Rogers, R. (1992) *Stories of Childhood*, Hemel Hempstead: Harvester Wheatsheaf.

Stevenson, O. (1989) *Age and Vulnerability: A Guide to Better Care*, London: Edward Arnold.

Stuart-Hamilton, I. (1994) *The Psychology of Ageing*, 2nd edn, London: Jessica Kingsley.

Szinovacz, M. (ed.) (1982) *Women's Retirement: Policy Implications of Recent Research*, London: Sage.

Taylor, D. (1989) 'Citizenship and Social Power', *Critical Social Policy* 26.

Thompson, N. (1989) 'Understanding Their Past and Family Life', *Community Care*, 25 May.

Thompson, N. (1991) *Crisis Intervention Revisited*, Birmingham: Pepar.

Thompson, N. (1992a) *Existentialism and Social Work*, Aldershot: Avebury.

Thompson, N. (1992b) 'Age and Citizenship', *Elders: The Journal of Care and Practice* 1(1).

Thompson, N. (1993) *Anti-Discriminatory Practice*, London: Macmillan.

Thompson, N. (1994a) *The Value Base of Social and Health Care*, Wrexham: Prospects Training Publications.

Thompson, N. (1994b) 'The Ontology of Masculinity', Paper presented at the Helping the Bereaved Male conference, London, Ontario, Canada, May.

Thompson, N. (1995a) 'Men and Anti-Sexism', *British Journal of Social Work*, 25(4).

Thompson, N. (1995b) *Theory and Practice in Health and Social Welfare*, Buckingham: Open University Press.

Thompson, N., Murphy, M. and Stradling, S. (1994) *Dealing with Stress*, London: Macmillan.

Thompson, S. and Thompson, N. (1993) *Perspectives on Ageing: Old Age in the Traditions of Social Thought*, Norwich: University of East Anglia Social Work Monographs.

Tinker, A. (1992) *Elderly People in Modern Society*, 3rd edn, London: Longman.

Totman, R. (1990) *Mind, Stress and Health*, London: Souvenir Press.

Townsend, P. (1986) 'Ageism and Social Policy', in Phillipson and Walker (1986).

Townsend, P. and Davidson, N. (1987) *Inequalities in Health*, Harmondsworth: Penguin.

Twelvetrees, A. (1991) *Community Work*, 2nd edn, London: Macmillan.

UPIAS (1976) *Fundamental Principles of Disability*, London: Union of the Physically Impaired Against Segregation.

Victor, C. (1991) *Health and Health Care in Later Life*, Milton Keynes: Open University Press.

Victor, C. (1994) *Old Age in Modern Society*, 2nd edn, London: Chapman and Hall.

Index

Developing Skills for Community Care

A collaborative approach

Peter Beresford and Steve Trevillion

Fundamental reforms in community care and welfare generally, demand new skills, new ways of working and a new relationship with service users. Collaboration is a key idea at the heart of this cultural change. Until now, there has been little guidance to help practitioners turn the rhetoric into reality. For the first time, this book offers a practical basis for working in a collaborative way, which fully involves service users.

Drawing on a development project which included service users, carers, practitioners and managers, the book pioneers a collaborative approach to developing collaborative skills. It takes the reader through the processes involved and identifies essential skills. Key questions like: • What are collaborative skills? • How can they be evaluated? • What would a bottom-up approach to skill development look like? are answered through numerous examples and exercises.

Peter Beresford works with Open Services Project, is a member of Survivors Speak Out and teaches at Brunel University College.
Steve Trevillion is a former neighbourhood social worker who now teaches at Brunel University College.

1995   173 pages   Hbk   1 85742 236 8   £32.50
Pbk   1 85742 237 6   £14.95

Price subject to change without notification

arena

Personal Safety for Social Workers

Pauline Bibby

Commissioned by
The Suzy Lamplugh Trust
Foreword by
Diana Lamplugh OBE

This book is aimed at employers, managers and staff in social work agencies.

In part 1, *Personal Safety for Social Workers* deals with the respective roles and responsibilities of employers and employees are discussed, and offers guidance on developing a workplace personal safety policy. The design and management of the workplace are considered and guidelines provided for social workers working away from the normal work base. Part 2 contains detailed guidelines for use by individual social workers in a variety of work situations. Part 3 addresses training issues and provides a number of sample training programmes.

The message of this book is that proper attention to risk can reduce both the incidence of aggression and its development into violent acts.

1994   224 pages   1 85742 195 7   £16.95

Price subject to change without notification

arena

Caring for Older Europeans

Comparative studies in 29 countries

George Giacinto Giarchi

This book provides a unique reference source covering the various modes of care (both formal and informal) of the elderly throughout Europe. This is applied to 29 countries of greater Europe rather than just the European Union: Northern Europe: Iceland, Finland, Norway, Sweden, Denmark; Western Europe: The Republic of Ireland, The UK, The Netherlands, Belgium, France, Luxembourg; Central Europe: Switzerland, Austria, Germany; Eastern Europe: The Czech and Slovak Republics, Bulgaria, The Commonwealth of Independent States, Poland, Hungary, Romania; Southern Europe: Italy, Spain, Portugal, Greece, The former Yugoslavia, Albania, Malta, Turkey, Cyprus.

Each chapter covers demography, the sociopolitical and administrative background, social security, pensions and benefits, housing provision, health care provision, mental health care, institutional care, personal social services, voluntary care agencies and support organizations, informal care, leisure and education, and rural aspects.

1996   596 pages   Hbk   1 85742 229 5   c £35.00
Pbk   1 85742 230 9   c £19.95

Price subject to change without notification

arena

COMMUNITY CARE:

NEW AGENDAS AND CHALLENGES FROM THE UK AND OVERSEAS

EDITED BY

David Challis
Bleddyn Davies
& Karen Traske

This book contains essays by many of the leading experts on community care from gerontology, medicine and related fields in the UK, continental Europe, and the USA. Among others, the authors include Sir Roy Griffiths, David Challis, Bleddyn Davies, Shah Ebrahim, Carrolle Estes (USA), Adalbert Evers (Germany), Janet Finch, Nori Graham, Jean-Claude Henrard (France), Kees Knipscheer (The Netherlands), Karen Luker, Matts Thorslund (Sweden) and Josh Wiener (USA).

The book both discusses current reforms in the UK and elsewhere, and illustrates what the research evidence shows to be the nature of the problems and how much the reforms could contribute to solving them. The subjects covered are among the key issues: empowerment and choice, the failings of the old system and how they are being introduced in the new system; the support of carers; new results from projects on care management and assessment, and the nature of the assessment being undertaken; lessons for the financing of community and continuing care and the mixing of the economy of care from the USA and other countries; and the impact of the health service changes.

1994   336 pages   Hbk   1 85742 208 2   £35.00

Price subject to change without notification

arena